I0807448

Historic Canada

East Saint John

On Sunday, August 4, 1996, a 24-inch water main burst on Rothesay Avenue in front of Centennial Motors and the Works Department garage. Water engineer Peter Hanlon was first on the scene to see the buckled pavement and the cars under water. The flood stretched from the post office to Russell Street. It took the Saint John Water Department staff just over a day to repair the break. After the clean-up, the smart staff at Centennial posted a sign with this message: "The Water Is Gone, Insurance Settled. Flood Sale Now On." (Peter Hanlon.)

On the Cover: The only entrance to East Saint John when this photograph was taken was over the Marsh Creek Bridge. Thorne Avenue runs to the right and Rothesay Avenue is at the left. (Heritage Resources 4455.)

Historic Canada

EAST SAINT JOHN

David Goss and Harold E. Wright

ARCADIA PUBLISHING

ISBN 978-0-7385-7394-6

Published by Arcadia Publishing
Charleston, South Carolina

Printed in the United States of America

Library of Congress Control Number: 2010930236

For all general information, please contact Arcadia Publishing:
Telephone 843-853-2070
Fax 843-853-0044
E-mail sales@arcadiapublishing.com
For customer service and orders:
Toll-Free 1-888-313-2665

Visit us on the Internet at www.arcadiapublishing.com

We dedicate this book to war veteran Art Pottle, in tribute to his long years of sharing his stories and in recognition that he has been an inspiration to many Saint Johners, serving his community in many ways. It is our hope that this collection will keep alive the story of the East Saint John that Art knew.

Contents

ACKNOWLEDGMENTS

We wish to thank the following people and organizations for providing photographs, information, and other assistance to us for this book: Al Phinney, Anita Grearson, Arthur Pottle, Bill Thompson, Bruce Carter, Caroline Smith, City of Saint John, Cliff Boyer, Crosby Molasses Company Ltd., David Goss, Don Collins, Fernhill Cemetery, Greg Marquis, Harold E. Wright, Jim Dixon, Jim Mollins, John Ellefson, Lois Ellis, Margo Mapplebeck, Pam Milne-Vincent, Peter Hanlon, Peter Kent, Provincial Archives of New Brunswick, Roly MacIntyre, Shane Hanson, Shearwater Aviation Museum, Terry and Mercer Munn, Val Ward, Victor Parker, Warren Harris, and Yves Leger; from Heritage Resources, Saint John (HR) collection: Al MacPherson, Andrea Bona, Arnold Buck, Beatrice Smith, Brenans Funeral Home, Canavan family, Charlie Stevens, Clow Canada, Col. J. G. Hart, Connie Marr, Doug Ferris, Doug McKay, E. C. Stewart, Emily Cannon, Evelyn Haeber, Fraser Beman, Freeland "Buzz" DeVenne, Garnet Phinney, George Pottle, Gerry Arrowsmith, Gerry McLaughlin, Gladys Donovan, Harold McKay, Jennie Arbo, Joan Alarie, Katheline Callaghan, Marion Lewis, Melissa Woodcock, Muriel Howard, Nick Skinner, Paul James, Phil Letson, Roly Wasson, Ron Jordon, Sally Jackson, Shirley Baxter, Shirley Whitneck, Starkey family, Stu Trentkowsky, Tracy Evans, Thelma Worden, Vince Richards, Virginia Dunbrack, and Walter Donnelly.

INTRODUCTION

The history of East Saint John is just as exciting and important as that of the rest of Saint John. It is unfortunate that it has been virtually ignored until now. Few know that part of East Saint John was once called Crouchville. The area east of the Marsh Creek Bridge and the Courtenay Bay Causeway is in itself made up of many smaller communities—Torryburn, Brookville, Coldbrook, Loch Lomond, Silver Falls, Lakewood, Golden Grove, Red Head, Mispec, and Willow Grove. Places or names like the Frog Pond, Tisdale Corner, and Courtenay are long gone. Rothesay Avenue was once known as the Post Road or the Great Marsh Road. Few probably know that Dorchester Penitentiary began as the St. John Penitentiary on the Red Head Road, now known as Bayside Drive. How many know that one of the world's most famous fossils was discovered at Silver Falls?

The area from Westmorland Road to Grandview Avenue had a wide mixture of industries: Foley Pottery, Lanergans and Lees brickyards, the glass works, the match plant, and of course, farms—so many farms. Next to these industries were the Alms House, the penitentiary, and later, the TB hospital, Willet Fruit, McMillan Paper, and then the dry dock. The Irving family interests have provided employment to thousands for decades. There were two industries that stand out. These were the McAvity Foundry and the dry dock. Together they gave work to tens of thousands of Saint Johners over the lives of their operations. The SuperStore and Staples were built on the site of McAvitys, but a drive down Bayside Drive still reveals the graving docks of the shipyard. Saint John's two attempts at automobile assembly were here, at the Coldbrook plant of J. A. Pugsley, where they assembled the Singer Six and, in the 1970s, the Bricklin in Grandview Avenue Industrial Park.

East Saint John was the place of some of the elegant homes of the 19th century—Craigie Lea, Woodside, Woodlawn, Nithbank, and Rockaway Cottage, which later became the site of the dry dock. The Great Marsh Road was the site of the One Mile House and, halfway down, the Two Mile House, finishing at the Frog Pond Tavern, later known as the Three Mile House. The military made their presence known at Torryburn and Red Head during the 19th century and during World War II, at Fort Mispec and at Coldbrook. The members of the Jervis Bay Legion, named after the famous World War II armed merchant cruiser, have helped keep alive the story of one of the greatest naval engagements of all time. There were so many schools: Latimore Lake, Lakewood, Woodlawn, East Saint John, Grandview Avenue, Simonds Jr. (now Bayview), Simonds Regional High (now Bayside), Simonds High, Champlain Heights, Forest Hills, Glen Falls, and Mispec. Many started as one-room schools that expanded as the neighbourhood did. Sadly, most of these are now closed.

Ben Lomond overlooks the Loch Lomond Lakes and its watershed. These lakes provide Saint John with much of its drinking water, and the story of this massive public works project is a book in itself. For most of the 19th and early 20th centuries, fishing and hunting guides took locals and visitors to the area for trout, salmon, and black bear.

Unlike the other areas of Saint John, there were no "great" fires, so many of the heritage buildings in the city have survived in East Saint John. Unlike the other areas of the city, these heritage buildings have not benefited from grants or assistance from city hall. One organization in the city today that has made tremendous strides in protecting the natural heritage of the east side is the Atlantic Coastal Action Program (ACAP). Their initiatives for Marsh Creek and its tributaries will one day result in a waterway without contaminants and with no odour. Although the smell from the creek today can be quite nasty, it is not like anything from the 1950 and 1960s. Once the government of Simonds Parish declared a state of emergency because of this problem, closing down industries, businesses, and schools. Maybe that was the inspiration for Saint John Common Council always looking at putting its sewerage treatment plants on the east side.

The stories and photographs that follow only touch the surface of this tremendous history. You will not find every story or answers to all your questions. We hope it will inspire you to ask questions of your parents and grandparents, your neighbours and friends. You can discover some of the history secrets of East Saint John. Perhaps we may be able to do a second volume on this tremendous part of our great city of Saint John.

Both of your authors are more familiar with the Uptown, North End, and the West Side. We thought it was appropriate to leave the last few paragraphs to a gentleman who has lived in the east side for much of his life, and who was honoured to serve as your member in the Legislative Assembly, Roly MacIntyre. Roly wrote the following:

> In reflecting on the east side, there are several outstanding people who come to mind. One is Jack Matthews from Red Head, who has long since passed away. He worked all day as a longshoreman and he also fished for lobster and salmon. He was well-known and well liked as a bit of a character and he was a good friend.
>
> The Simonds Arena brings back many memories. It was the home of minor hockey and I was the president for quite a few years. I spent many years at the ANE [Atlantic National Exhibition] working in the hockey fundraising booth. It was a sad day when the arena was demolished. We used to have hundreds of kids playing baseball in East Saint John. As a coach for the Little League and as president of East Suburban Little League in the 1970s, it was exciting to see so many young people from our area participating and competing in organized sports.
>
> Anna (Graham) Boyle, the matriarch of the west side Boyle family, was raised at Grahams Brooke near Loch Lomond. She knew most of the companies and many of the families who lived in the area. When we talked about the match factory, she said that her sister had worked there for many years. She is very excited about this book about East Saint John.
>
> Even though I have lived out east for 34 years, I was not aware of the in-depth history of our area. Over the years I have heard many stories and this book holds a wealth of well researched information. It will bring back many memories to those who have lived in the Saint John area.

One

The Parish of Simonds

This 1899 view from atop Reeds Folly on Mount Pleasant Avenue reveals an East Saint John that is no more. In the background are the trees of Forest Hills. Marsh Creek and the Great Marsh Road (Rothesay Avenue) are at the left, and at the far right is Courtenay Bay. The Church of England Burying Ground on Thorne Avenue is to the right of centre. (HR1877.)

This view looks toward Rothesay Avenue from the roof of the Saint John General Hospital. In the foreground is Haymarket Square, where many businesses were located that served East Saint Johners. After World War II, the business community began to spread to the east. In this 1960 view, Dominion Store is under construction on the right and a new liquor is behind the Texaco at Cooper's Corner; McAvity's smokestack has been removed as part of the area change. (HR2406.)

A *c.* 1960 reverse view of Cooper's Corner looks toward the city, with the 1932 General Hospital atop Vinegar Hill. This corner was the only entrance to the city centre from the east. On the left, the East End barracks are being torn down for the new Dominion Store, and on the right at Seaton Street is Crystal Ice, who, with Crosby Molasses, was then about to manufacture Sky detergent at this site. (HR7758.)

In the foreground of this 1863 view of Courtenay Bay, a ship is under construction, and the workers would have lived in the homes between the yard and the Cathedral of the Immaculate Conception at the top of the hill. Until Stella Maris Church was built on Bayside Drive in 1924, Roman Catholics in East Saint John were likely to attend the cathedral. Other spiritual homes show up in chapter two. (HR10008.)

Shipbuilding had been this area's main 19th-century commercial enterprise during the era of tall ships. The last two wooden ships built in Saint John were constructed in Courtenay Bay. In 1918 and 1919, the ships *War Fundy* and *War Moncton* were built in the Grant and Horne Yard with over 150 on the job. The *Moncton* was launched in May 1919 for the Imperial Munitions Board but did not see war service. (HR4516.)

The defence of a city that had shipbuilding capabilities, munitions factories, and a thriving port used for shipping goods to the war zone in Europe required the presence of the military. Many of the men and women were stationed in the east end. In 1941, Defence Minister Ralston visited the 8th antiaircraft battery at the East End Grounds and was watched intently by a curious kid from nearby Thorne Avenue. (HR1155.)

McAvity's began business as hardware merchants in 1833 and moved into manufacturing valves and hydrants, becoming known internationally for their expertise and quality products. When the American military were looking for an out-of-country munitions manufacturing location, they turned to Saint John and the McAvity industrialists. In five months, they built the huge plant on Rothesay Avenue in 1916. These men were working the "rough turn section" for 9.2-inch shells. (HR7172.)

The Great Fire of 1877 did not directly affect East Saint John, as the area was farmland and wilderness when that catastrophic event occurred. However, as will be seen in chapter nine, the scourge of fire visited the area on many occasions and engulfed more than a few of the homes and commercial structures that were built over the years. This fire occurred in May 1976 at McKnight Motors, 567 Rothesay Avenue. (HR8272.)

Tuberculosis was a little understood disease when a hospital for those fighting the infection was established off Bayside Drive, then still a very rural east in December 1915. Fresh air and quiet were considered as important as any medicine at that time, thus the location for the 50-patient hospital, which eventually had 200 patients. Further views of this landmark East Saint John building will be seen in chapter two. (HR11088.)

The Saint John County Hospital opened in December 1915 for the treatment of tuberculosis patients. It was enlarged in 1918 by the Department of Soldier's Civil Re-establishment. In 1919, a children's wing was built and the Nesbitt Wing for children added in 1930. The name of the hospital was changed to the Saint John Tuberculosis Hospital in 1929 and, in 1962, to the East Saint John Hospital. It closed in 1976. (HR13144.)

On Dominion Day 1893, Lady Alice Tilley's idea of a home for wayward boys became a reality with the opening of the Boy's Industrial Home on 40 acres of farmland on the Red Head Road. From its inception as a training aid, and to augment food supplies, there were horses, pigs, chickens, and cows, as seen being milked here. The home closed in 1962 when Kingsclear opened near Fredericton. (HR5790.)

When Turnbull Field in Clover Valley, Loch Lomond, opened in January of 1952, air travel was a new way of transportation to the average Saint Johner, and the airfield personnel undertook the task of informing the public of the opportunity for flights to far-off locations with a series of air shows and displays of aircraft at the new facility. (HR6078.)

In 1950, this family from Prince Street West enjoyed their picnic at Mispec Beach on makeshift tables in front of the Royal Canadian Navy building left over from World War II. This structure served the community well as a dance hall and canteen over the years, but the current building now needs replacing. Today few people picnic on the beach, most opting for the more traditional sunbathing. (HR12875.)

Two

Caring and Learning in the Benevolent Past

As people moved east, they chose to live in subdivisions built on the farmlands in and around Crouchville. There was soon a need for schools, churches, and social institutions. This 1942 view shows the land on Bayside Drive adjacent the dry dock used for the poorhouse at the left and the Boys Industrial Home and TB hospital at the right. In the background are East Saint John School and Stella Maris Church. (HR1616.)

In 1842, the city transferred its poorhouse from King Street East to Bayside Drive. The five-storey brick building housed inmates who were unable to care for themselves. In later years, the poorhouse was called the Municipal Home, and the grounds included a large and productive farm with many purebred animals. Despite this, one resident described the food as "three meals of thin gruel a day with an onion twice a week and half a roll on Sundays." The home had its own graveyard. In 1942, the modern firefighting apparatus included the "novel chutes," shown in the photographs, to assure a quick exit. (Above, HR11953; below, HR10855.)

Every summer, the bishop of Saint John hosted a children's picnic at his summer residence in Torryburn. In 1934, the parade was led by the City Cornet Band, via Mill Street, en route to Union Station, where they boarded the train for Torryburn. Through the afternoon, the children played games and enjoyed typical picnic treats and a concert by the Cornet Band before returning to their homes in the city. (HR275.)

Behind St. Joachim's Church at Silver Falls stood St. Patrick's Industrial Home (above). In 1879, Bishop Sweeney bought land for an orphanage and farm. The building was 90 feet by 50 feet and accommodated 150 boys. The upper storey was the dorm, the second storey was for staff, and the ground floor was for reception, class, and study rooms as well as the chapel, as captured in this 1941 photograph (below) by Sr. L. S. The farm was 100 acres, and the bishop expected the boys to raise enough food for their own consumption. The total cost of the orphanage was $10,000, of which $7,000 came from Squire Patrick McCourt, an Irish mason. A fair was held at St. Malachi's hall in October 1879 to raise the remaining funds to complete the school. Probably the most famous resident was Canadian folk legend Stompin' Tom. (Above, HR12182; below, HR3739.)

In 1923 and 1924, the John Flood Company built the Stella Maris Church on Bayside Drive. There are two rather unusual tidbits to the story of this church. One is that some of the construction material came from the nearby Saint John Penitentiary, then part of the Boy's Industrial Home. The second is that the church bell was originally the Labour's Bell from Market Slip. It was given to the church in memory of the labourers of the city. (Don Collins.)

This 1923 view of the first Woodlawn School does not reveal anything of the significant history of this site or name. Woodlawn was the family home of the Tisdale family, one of the earliest property owners in this area. By 1875, the homestead was also the site of a military powder magazine. The school shown here was replaced by a modern elementary school in 1950 that closed in June 1995. It reopened as the Woodlawn Learning Centre in September 1999. (HR9817.)

With River Avenue in the foreground, this 1950s view of the East Saint John School shows the prominent place it had overlooking Bayside Drive near the dry dock. During World War II a temporary anti-aircraft gun was sited near the school. After the school closed in the early 2000s, it was purchased and sensitively renovated for office space by one of the Irving Companies. (HR10853.)

Eighth-grade boys in East Saint John School, 1943, are, from left to right, (first row) James Belding, Richard Simpson, Roger Fleiger, Frank Lawson, and Harold Magee; (second row) Donald McGaghy and Andrew Simpson (from England); (third row) Eddie Golding, Bert Forgey, Everett Dunning, John R. Glaspy, Wally Boudreau, Perry Craft, and James "Red" Cassidy. (HR9715.)

The two-storey Glen Falls School was built in 1918 on 7.5 acres of land donated by the Glen Falls Development Company. In the early years, there were about 72 students, but as the Glen Falls subdivision grew, so did the demand for an expanded school. Between 1939 and 1948, six classrooms were added to the original building. Flooding was always a problem, and in 1951 the water rose to the bottom of the first floor. The old school was demolished in July 1975. (Val Ward.)

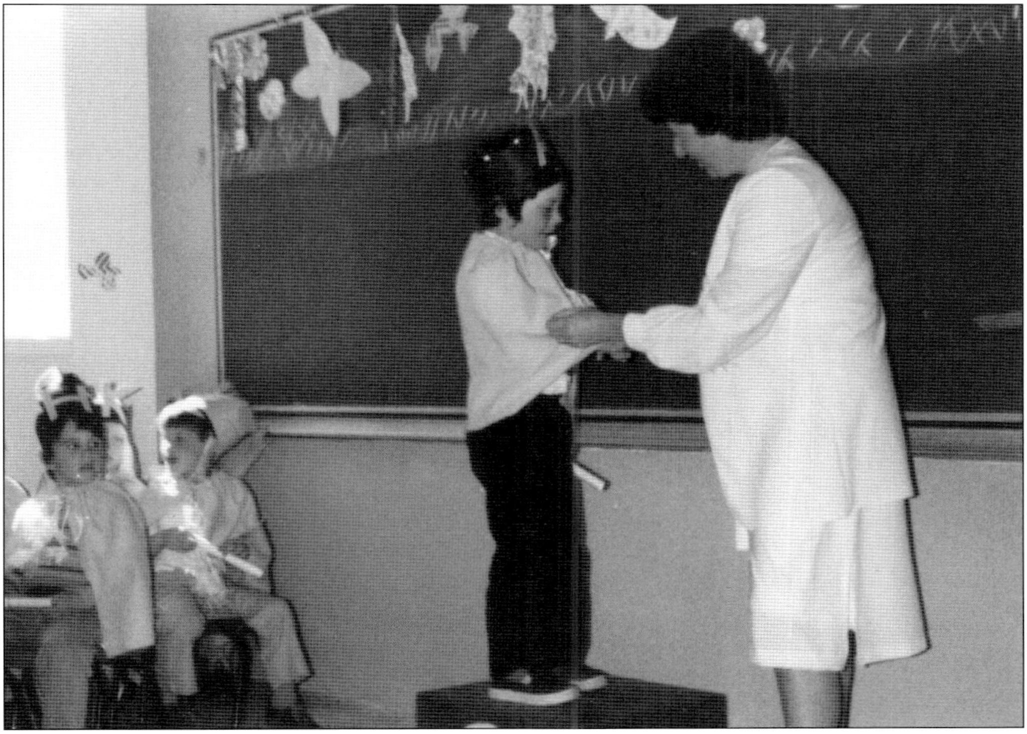

Five-year-old Andy Munn is being congratulated by his kindergarten teacher, Mrs. McCormick, at the new Glen Falls School in June 1982. Andy attended this school to grade 7 and then spent grades 8 to 11 in school in Peace River, Alberta. He then took a year off and was in Australia on behalf of the Rotary Club of Canada. Andy returned to grade 12 in Athabasca, Alberta, but his life was cut short in an automobile accident in February 1995. (Terry Munn.)

In 1913, architect F. Neil Brodie drew up plans for a wood-framed tuberculosis hospital on Douglas Avenue. The public rejected that site; the plans were adapted to brick; and a 60-bed, $125,000 structure was built on municipal land off Bayside Drive. It opened on December 9, 1915, with Dr. H. A. Farris as resident superintendent at a yearly salary of $1,500. Carrie Hall was the matron–head nurse at $600 annually. (HR5608.)

On December 28, 1954, this portrait of Dr. H. A. Farris was unveiled to mark his 39 years as superintendent at the institution. His work had borne much fruit over the many years, though tuberculosis was still a threat to many lives. In this photograph are, from left to right, J. Marcel Gatien; Robert McAllister, MLA; warden Ernest A. Whitebone; Dr. E. W. Lunney; and Dr. R. J. Collins. The current whereabouts of this painting are unknown. (HR3752.)

"Children first" was an early motto of those fighting tuberculosis, and an effort was made to check city children for the disease at free clinics offered by nurses of the institution. Those requiring a hospital stay, however, had no special quarters until 1930, when Montreal businessman Arthur J. Nesbitt financed construction of a 52-patient wing for children shown here enjoying a rhythm band practice just as they would in regular school classes. One benefit of the Nesbitt wing was a shorter patient stay, in addition to the opportunity to treat more children. Several years before the Nesbitt Wing was constructed, the Imperial Order Daughters of the Empire (IODE) had undertaken to finance teachers, which helped the patients to keep up with their schooling during their hospital stay. The hospital was accredited by the American College of Surgeons, and was the only TB hospital in North America to be recognized. (Above, HR5607; left, HR5606.)

As treatment methods changed over the years, new equipment was added to assist in the fight against tuberculosis. In 1918, an ambulance and an X-ray machine were added, a Ford truck replaced an aged horse, and a library for patients was started. The children in this 1960s photograph benefited from these additions and also the latest treatments in the fight against TB. (HR13005.)

An unknown child, likely a family visitor, enjoys an ice cream at the TB hospital lawn party, the highlight of the summer for TB patients. These parties were originally organized by Charlie Jones, shown standing left, for the Knights of Pythias, whose members, as well as their wives and Pythian Sisters, served sandwiches and provided the entertainment on the lawn of the hospital. (HR9154.)

The long days and nights of enforced rest at the TB hospital were broken up to some degree by various forms of entertainment. The first was in 1919, when F. G. Spencer, a Saint John moviehouse owner, provided a moving picture machine for the free use of the patients. An August 9, 1948, article in the *Evening Times Globe* described the annual summer entertainment, known as the Good Cheer Picnic, and notes the patients were wheeled out into a "large hollow square" and a "stage was set up, and entertainers performed." Among those performers on that occasion, fairly typical of all the others held over the years, were pianist Harry Brown, vocalist Viola Day, singer Fred Jones, step dancer John Bundy, and Herb Nelly, impersonator, to name just a few, some of whom may be in the photograph below. (Above, HR9189; below, HR9155.)

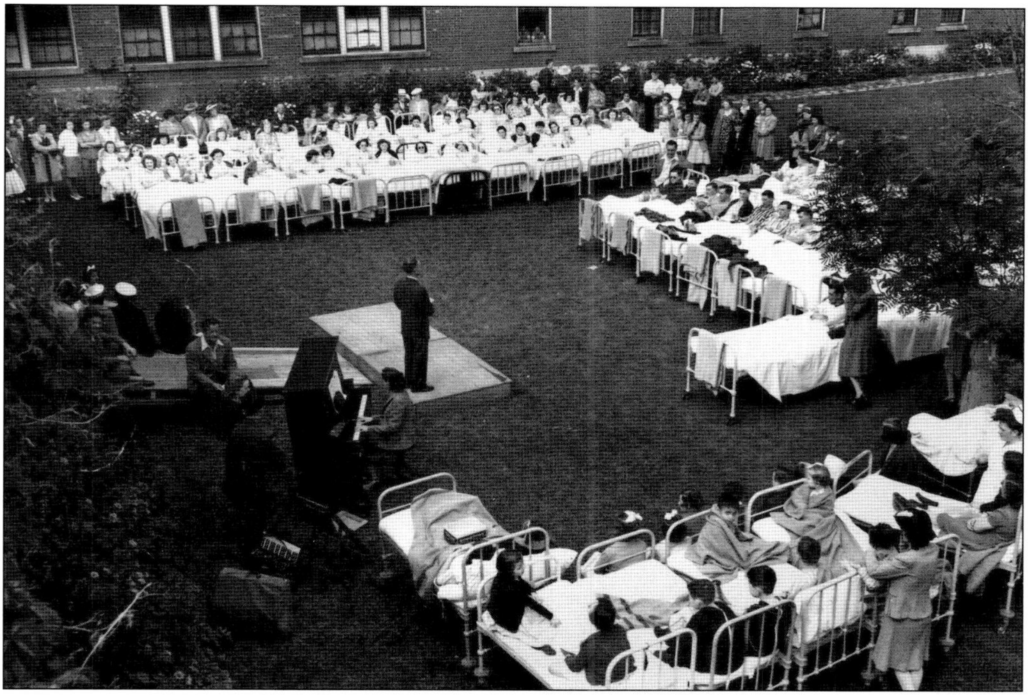

A home for delinquent boys in Saint John was opened in 1893 on what was then known as Red Head Road. It was described as a handsome brick building with airy rooms. There was a schoolroom for 30 students, a dining room that would seat 150, and it was noted that the setting in "99 cases out of 100" would be better than the home from which the boys came. (HR5680.)

Shown here is the Boys Industrial Home and its barns and outbuildings, as viewed from the rear of East Saint John School. Initially built for 45 inhabitants, at times it held almost double that number. Despite encroaching neighbourhoods and changing times, the institution survived for 69 years. It was described as "long outdated" when it was closed in December 1962, and the 55 boys still institutionalized were transferred to Kingsclear, outside of Fredericton. (HR5787.)

When the facility opened in 1893, it was normal for institutions like as the Boys Industrial Home to have adjacent gardens and provisions for caring for livestock on their grounds. The superintendent's 1931 report noted, "in spite of our lack of acreage . . . the farm is our best source of Vocational Training." An added bonus was that quantities of food were produced to help with the costs of running such institutions. (HR5803.)

The 1931 report commented on the livestock program at the institution, noting there was "sufficient butter for home use" and "sufficient milk for boys and staff." Of the cattle, it said, "our young stock are in favourable demand by farmers throughout the province for breeding purposes." As only the older boys could work with the cattle, there were 700 poultry with which "smaller boys can be actively engaged." (HR5793.)

In October 1951, members of the IODE continued their long tradition of support to the patients of the TB hospital by presenting a framed photograph of King George VI and Queen Elizabeth to the kindergarten teacher of the day, Jean Taylor. Without volunteer assistance, the life of those in the hospital, the municipal home, the penitentiary, and the Boys Industrial Home would have been much bleaker. (HR5789.)

Three

The City of the Dead

Established in 1848 in wilderness off Marsh Road, the Rural Cemetery was the name of this property until 1899. Over 39,814 remains lie in the "City of Sleep," and there is still room for another century of burials in the 200 acres of rolling hillside. Near this rest house are two Fathers of Confederation; Kilby Reynolds, builder of the Reversing Falls Bridge in 1853; and Winnifred (Blair) Drummie, the country's first Miss Canada in 1923. (Fernhill Cemetery.)

Fernhill Cemetery began with the purchase of 70 acres of land from James Peters Jr. in 1847. Saint John architect Matthew Stead laid out the cemetery, and his work can still be enjoyed to this day when walking the rambling, tree-studded pathways that give the area its park-like and peaceful atmosphere. The shelter shown here was built in 1883. Nellie Jones (left) is standing at the iron gate, installed in 1874, at the now closed Rothesay Avenue entrance. A second ornate rest house was built in 1898 and restored in 1991. The September 1945 military funeral of Lt .Col. Reginald L. H. Goodday (below) was held from St. Paul's Anglican Church in Rothesay to burial in Lot 5760, grave 2, at Fernhill. (Left, HR8998; below, HR11272.)

When the cemetery first opened, it was common for plot owners to come annually to clean up the grounds, straighten the stones, and plant flowers for their loved ones. An omnibus service ran from King's Square to the cemetery to assist those travelling. A picnic would be packed to enjoy at the ornate pavilion, where Margaret Milne (right) posed in the 1930s. She may have seen the Brennan's glass hearse shown in the photograph below or one similar to it. The first such hearse was introduced by undertaker Mark N. Powers at his Princess Street funeral home between 1846 and 1857. (Right, Pam Milne-Vincent; below, HR9964.)

Among the aesthetic improvements to the grounds over the years were the planting of elm trees at the main entrance in 1898, flower beds established at the new entrance from Westmorland Road to the South Road in 1898, and the eastern portion of the cemetery given over to cultivation of wildflowers in 1909. Despite the Depression, in 1933 perennial flowers and shrubs were added to a new rockery walk along South Drive. Such beautification has continued to modern times. In 1966, five Canadian maples were planted to mark Canada's centennial and 10 Miss Canada rose bushes added to the 235 in the cemetery at the time. The duck pond (above), no longer part of the City of the Dead, was put in before 1917 and was still there in 1966. Margaret Milne (left) was related by marriage to the Clayton family, who were the cemetery caretakers. (Above, HR-Wright; left, Pam Milne-Vincent.)

The Naval and Military Lot, now known as the Field of Honour, was established by the IODE in 1915. On November 7, 1915, Pvt. James S. Brown became the first soldier interred. The Field of Honour contains 412 burials. The Commonwealth War Graves Commission cares for 103 foreign and non–world war burials in this cemetery. (Fernhill Cemetery.)

On August 14, 1902, the Knights of Pythias held their first Decoration Day at the cemetery when they laid wreaths on the graves of departed members. Chief among these was the founder of the knights, John Beamish, who formed the New Brunswick Lodge No. 1 on October 28, 1870. He died in 1919, and the memorial stone that tells his story was placed as part of Decoration Day in 1923. (HR9223.)

Those living in proximity to Fernhill have long enjoyed strolling in the park-like surroundings and often stopped to take photographs of the decorative elements. Posed at left on the giant anchor in the seafarers Marine Lot are, from left to right, Gertrude (Berteit) Milne, Margaret Milne, Val Brodersen, and her brother Thor. In more recent times, Walk N' Talk programs have been held on a regular basis to acquaint the general public with the cemetery and the story of some of the more than 39,000 burials that have taken place there. Canada Day (Dominion Day was the original name) is one of those occasions. This is the only cemetery with two Fathers of Confederation burials. John Watson (below) is explaining how the United Empire Loyalist Society had undertaken the refurbishment of the Botsford family marker in order to keep the memory alive of a settler buried 150 years ago. (Left, Pam Milne-Vincent; below, H. E. Wright.)

Four

LOCH LOMOND

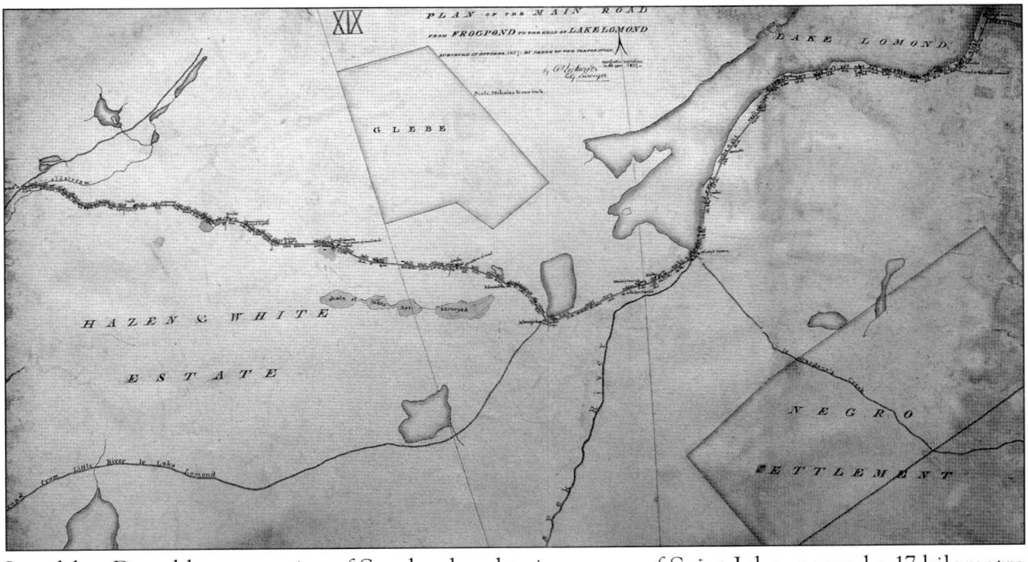

Lauchlan Donaldson, a native of Scotland and twice mayor of Saint John, named a 17-kilometre chain of lakes after his homeland's Loch Lomond. This 1827 map shows from the Frog Pond to the head of Lake Lomond, the black settlement at Willow Grove, and that a large part of the land was still held by the estate of loyalists Hazen and White. In 1855, the lakes became the city's water supply. (HR-Wright.)

City engineer William Murdock Jr. wrote in 1904 that black settlers had been originally granted a block of land consisting of 3,600 acres laid out in 50-acre lots about 1.5 kilometres from the large lake at Loch Lomond. Only about 500 of the acres were actually taken by blacks, he noted, and most of it is now in the "hand of whites," and "blacks have become scarce." Black settlers like Adam Hull, who drew lot 33 at Loch Lomond (below), received poor lands, little in the way of provisions to work the land, and led a tough life. The photograph above shows the recreated discovery of the remains of Maggie Vail. In 1868 her lover, John A. Munro, shot her and their child not far from the Willow Grove settlement. (Above, Provincial Archives; below, HR-Wright.)

Adam Hull
Drew Lot N°33 northside
affrican settlement
Loch Lomond

These photographs show the Roach family at Taylor Lake in Willow Grove, about 1935. They are, from left to right, George Hector, Clarence, Frances, Jimmy, Isabelle, May, and three unidentified grandchildren. Rosie Roach sits atop her pony. The black settlers did not prosper in the Willow Grove area, and the government of the time has to take a share of the blame. Not only were they given less land than white settlers and other immigrants, but they received the poorest land. By 1827, most were on assistance and receiving aid, especially to get through the long winter. A petition to establish a gristmill in the area fell on deaf ears. A study by W. A. Spray in *Acadiensis* laid out the story of the black settlers at Willow Grove and concluded, "the settlement . . . can only be viewed as a failure." (Above, HR4149; right, HR4132.)

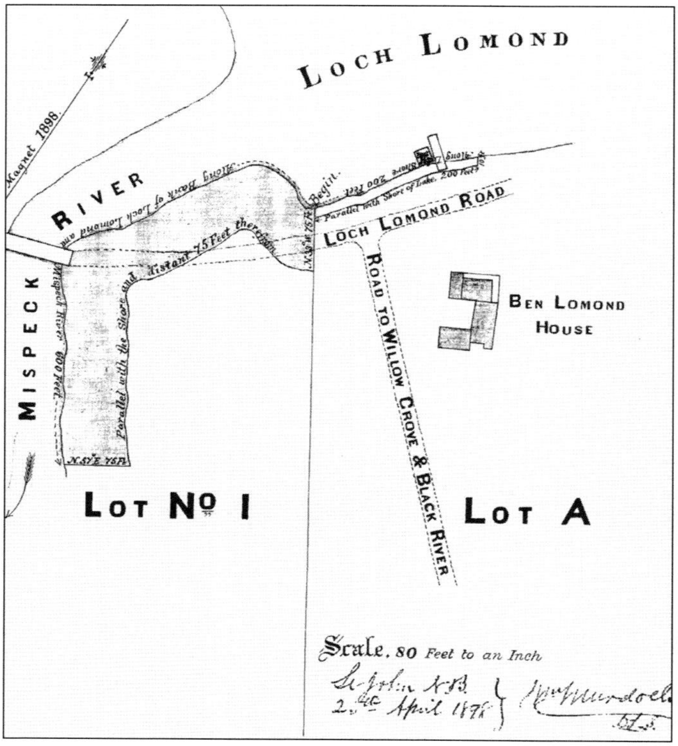

In a historical sketch written by LeBaron Jordan in 1950, he described Loch Lomond in the late 1700s as "wilderness" that was reached by a "foot path from Frog Pond" that ran 5 miles to the Loch Lomond Lakes. (Readers can refer to page 37 for a glimpse at the distances noted and to see that the footpath became the Loch Lomond Road.) This 1898 map (left) shows the road as it nears the main Loch Lomond Lake, with the Mispec River, which became the channel for the city's water supply, flowing out of the lake. Just behind the lake, on the road that leads to the black settlement at Willow Grove, is Ben Lomond House (below), a popular resort for sportsmen. (Left, Works Dept.; below, HR7727.)

This photograph of Loch Lomond was a surprise find, as it came from the scrapbook of a St. George native, Anita Grearson, who lives 100 kilometres from the lakes. Since 1855, this and other lakes in the 41-square-mile surrounding area, with a storage capacity of 80 million gallons, have been the city's water supply. Being 300 feet above sea level, the water flows naturally through pipes to the city. (Anita Grearson.)

In the late 19th and early 20th centuries, several hotels stood on the shores of Loch Lomond, catering to the fishermen (and fisherwomen) who flocked to the lakes, where landlocked salmon were the big attraction. This occurred as the lake's outfall at Mispec had been dammed for many years, and salmon could not come upriver to spawn or leave to go to sea. The Eckebrecht ladies had considerable success in 1909. Today there is little fishing on the lakes. (HR10390.)

From the time he discovered the beauty of the Loch Lomond Lakes, Lauchlan Donaldson encouraged others to visit the bucolic area, and some of those people took up permanent residence or opened lodges or hotels so that those who visited would have comfortable accommodations. Over the years, John Munroe and William George Cody built roadhouses; John Jordon operated a sawmill; and E. Sentell and many others farmed successfully and also did lumbering and shoe repair. Churches were built for Anglicans and Catholics; agricultural and temperance societies formed; military manoeuvres took place. Indeed Loch Lomond became a place to escape the city and while away the hours as the unidentified gent reposing on the watershed bridge did in 1903. Louis Eckebrecht (below) shows off his Otter Lake "catch of the day" in 1909. (Above, HR1699; below, HR10388.)

Five

Wings over Clover Valley

In 1954, Frank Ogden of Toronto landed his Mooney "wee scotsman" plane at Clover Valley. En route from Toronto to Newfoundland, he dropped in to visit members of the Fundy Flying Club. Club president Bruce Carter (center) lost no time in inspecting the world's smallest production line plane. At left is the wee one's owner, Frank Ogden, and on the right is Fred Hilton. In the background is a Trans Canada Airline (TCA) North Star. (HR-Carter.)

Among the first passengers to fly out of the new airport on January 1, 1952, was Premier J. B. McNair, en route to Jamaica, where he was a guest of Lord Beaverbrook. The premier was given best wishes for a safe flight by warden Arthur Carton and Charles R. Wasson, chairman of the airport commission. The premier's daughter Janet is at the foot of the stairs. TCA stewardess Mary McLeod, R.N., of Dominion, Nova Scotita, is at the top of the stairs of the DC-3 Skyliner. (HR2458.)

During Canada's centennial year, 1967, the Turnbull Field hosted another air show. The Royal Canadian Air Force (RCAF) Hercules C130E-LM, serial no. 10312 is on display in front of the terminal. This airplane went into service with the RCAF in March 1965 (being a former U.S. Air Force aircraft). When in Saint John, this plane was assigned to No. 436 (T) Squadron at Uplands in Ottawa. It crashed in Quebec in November 1980 while on a search, killing eight crewmembers. (HR11284.)

The July 1959 Air Show featured a wide range of activities for airplane aficionados and hundreds of families. There was a parachute drop by Floyd C. Martineau of Ontario, which almost ended in disaster; an RCAF Otter from No. 103 Search and Rescue Squadron; and the Argus and Neptune antisubmarine aircraft from Greenwood, Nova Scotia. A highlight of the day was the music from the RCAF Command Band. (HR-Carter.)

These airmen are disembarking from an RCAF Canadair North Star in preparation for the 1959 air show. This show was sponsored by the 250 (Saint John) Wing of the RCAF Association and the Fundy Flying Club. The show included jet fighters from Maine and the RCAF aerobatic team, the Golden Hawks. This aircraft joined the RCAF in 1947 and made at least one trip into Korea during that war. In 1966, the plane was sold to a company in Florida, where it was eventually scrapped. (HR-Carter.)

The new municipal airport, designated YSJ in airport language, welcomed its first passengers in August 1951 when Maritime Central Airways (MCA) moved their operations to Clover Valley. TCA moved their operations from Pennfield Ridge airport at the end of December 1951. It is a shame that these men, who worked for TCA in the mid-1950s, remain unidentified, although two of them may be W. J. Hegan and ramp agent/attendant Bob Anderson. (HR6077.)

YSJ airport manager Don Crookshank (left) and Dick Mollins, station manager for MCA, are pictured here in 1956. Don was the second airport manager (1953–1956), following in the footsteps of Bill Arrowsmith (1951–1953). Dick filled many roles for MCA—station manager, ticket seller, radio operator, and baggage handler. He remained with MCA until its sale to Eastern Provincial in 1963, when he went to work for the New Brunswick Telephone Company. (HR12238.)

This is one of the most famous and unusual airport visitors. Dick Mollins, the ticket agent at left, was quite pleased to meet and shake paws with this Hollywood celebrity. Down the aircraft stairs came Lassie, star of 20th-century movies, television, and the circus ring. Lassie was in the city for a performance of her "poisoned dog" trick at the Main Street Forum. CHSJ radio star Foster Marr presented Lassie with an engraved dog collar, making her a "Free Dog of the City." (HR11532.)

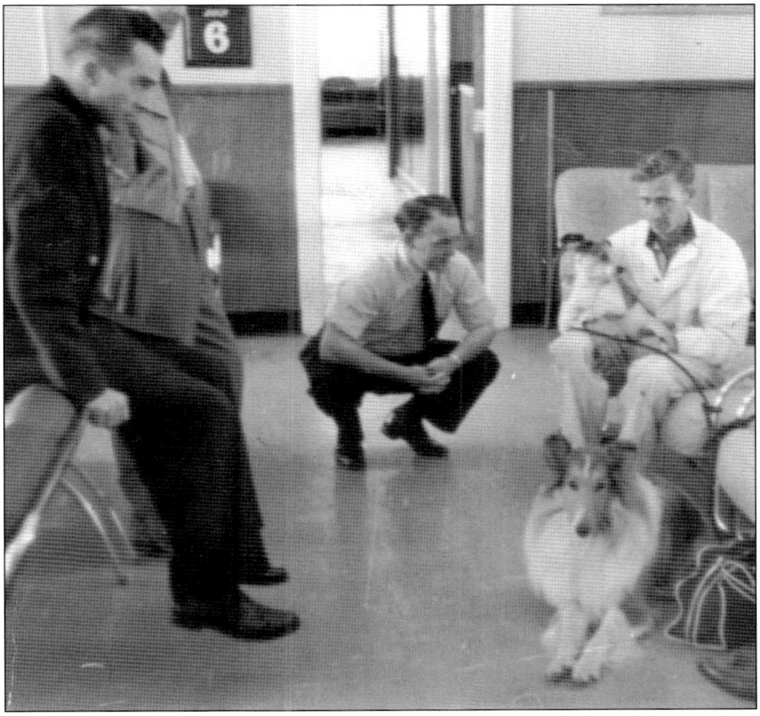

From 1951 to 1958, MCA's DC-3s loaded supplies from Fraser Brace and flew them to the Pine Tree radar sites in Labrador. There was considerable secrecy around this project. When the inaugural DC-3 arrived in 1951, the aircrew and passengers were met by an official welcoming party. According to the *Evening Times Globe*, a second DC-3 landed 15 minutes later that loaded supplies and 14 men and then left for a "secret" destination to "unload ships" for several months. (HR11545.)

There were only a few licensed female pilots in Saint John in the 1950s. From left to right, Doris Logan, Regina Jordan, and Lois Carvell soon joined the ranks of the flying women. Of the three, Gina Jordan went on to an illustrious flying career with over 18,000 flying hours. Gina trained air cadets at Greenwood and had her own flight school in Calgary. In 1981, she joined the Mission Aviation Fellowship, flying supplies to Zaire, Tanzania, and Madagascar. (HR-Ellis.)

West-sider Lois Carvell took her first flight in October 1955 aboard the Fundy Flying Club's Fleet CF-DZM, under the watchful eye of instructor Bruce Carter. She received her private pilot's license in August 1956. It was at the club that Lois met "Big Joe" Ellis, whom she married in 1976. Lois is at the controls of the club's Tri-Pacer CF-KRC, which was undergoing engine maintenance in the Fundy Flying Club's hangar. (HR-Ellis.)

Air cadet Tommy Enright and pilot Shirley Baxter are seen here at Milledgeville. Tommy took his training in 1948 under Bob Irwin and was licensed in 1949. Shirley was ready for a flight and asked Tommy if he wanted to be her passenger. The flying training was sponsored by the Royal Canadian Flying Clubs Association, the Air Cadet League of Canada and, in Saint John, the Fundy Flying Club. (HR-Baxter.)

Flying Club instructor Joe Ellis and son Paul of the 161 Air Cadets are pictured here. Paul received his private pilot license in 1955 and graduated from vocational school in 1956. He joined the RCAF shortly after and became a pilot in 1958. After serving with Fighter Group Headquarters at CFB North Bay, Ontario, Paul became the Canadian detachment commander at Tyndall Air Force Base, Florida, for the U.S. Air Force 23rd North American Aerospace Defense Command. (HR-Ellis.)

Pilot "Big Joe" Ellis (left) and photographer Lou Wilson are seen here prior to a flight where Lou would take photographs for a commercial client. Flights over the city were for clients like CHSJ radio, which had leaflets called "Watch the Sky at 11 o'clock" for a free television set. And then there are the photographs over the Nurses Residence on Waterloo Street, where Lou and Joe captured some of the nursing students on the roof sunbathing. (HR-Ellis.)

The search for a new municipal airport site began in 1943. Clover Valley was approved in 1944, and construction began in 1949. Jimmy Wade, one of Canada's most famous aviators, landed the first aircraft here in September 1949. The first scheduled flight into Saint John Airport (YSJ) was an MCA DC-3 in August 1951. The airport was officially opened on January 8, 1952. In 1961, the airport was renamed Turnbull Field for the inventor of the electric variable pitch propeller. (HR-Wright.)

Six

MISPEC ON THE FUNDY

The first land grants in Mispec were made in 1786 to loyalists John Thorp, Charles Shoonenwolf, and Samuel Moore. The land was unsuitable for farming, so the original grants were rescinded and, in 1821, were re-granted to loyalists Thomas Thomas, Christopher Smiler, and Job Standley. The ocean beach, shown here in 1942, became a popular attraction. In 1871, the village had a population of 200 and today serves as a semirural suburb for Saint John. (HR1627.)

There were two mills built over the Mispec River. The gang-sawmill, built between 1821 and 1829, made fish boxes. A wool and cotton mill was built by the St. John Manufacturing Company in 1861. Their products included wool knitting yarns and cotton warp in white, blue, red, orange, and green dyes. The mill used native wool with cotton imported from New York. These mills were gone by 1891 when a pulp mill was built. (HR8829.)

Frank Harris moved his family from Wales to Mispec in 1947. Lena and Frank are pictured with their children, from left to right, Caroline, Warren, and Brian. Noeline was later born here. Frank, a merchant mariner, visited during the war. Caroline remembers, "We finally came to the place that would be our home, there was nothing but alder bushes and a house under construction. Dad had even used theatre posters as wall covering. . . . There was no indoor plumbing and no electricity. We were to be pioneers in every sense of the word." (Harris family.)

The St. John Sulphite Company mill, owned by Scottish investors, was built and managed in 1898 by Michael Mooney. The dam for this mill was built of stone and faced with wood. This dam prevented salmon from spawning in the Mispec River, which was a source of dispute for many decades. The mill had a short operational life. By 1903, it was insolvent and the lease reverted to the city. (HR11926.)

The operation of the mill was taken over by Stetson and Cutler of Indiantown. They operated the mill from 1905 until 1920, when the facility was closed and demolished. Much of the building material was recycled into a new mill in Nova Scotia. In 1951, the City of Saint John sold 1,576 acres of Mispec River land, including the six mill staff residences on the hill above the structure. (HR6050.)

The remains of a fishing wharf at Thomas Creek are seen in this 1930 image. Fishing for salmon in the Mispec River and commercial fishing in the Bay of Fundy were mainstays of the local Mispec community for decades. Once a finger wharf went from being useful for fishermen, it usually became a popular attraction for visitors, as shown here for the photograph opportunity. (HR9884.)

The focus of the Thomas Creek fishing community in 1930 is evident—lobster traps and lots of them! For many Mispec lobstermen, this crustacean was a staple on their tables. As both domestic and international markets realized the value of this delicacy, the market for Mispec lobsters grew far and wide. Today fishermen use the wharf at the Mispec River for their operations. (HR9883.)

On a warm day in 1970, thousands of Saint Johners flocked to Fort Mispec for the opening of the Irving Canaport deepwater oil terminal. Ships laden with oil from all over the world were able to tie up to an offshore monobuoy and unload their cargo to be stored in the onsite storage tanks. Visitors were treated to Baxter's ice cream and other picnic treats while they were able to visit the ruins of the World War II fort. In 2009, the liquified natural gas (LNG) plant on site began operations. (HR11619.)

When Irving Oil began developing the site for Canaport, they made sure the concrete fortifications were safe for visitors. They provided park benches and some audio interpretation. In 1993, former gunners who served there with the 4th Heavy Battery during World War II revisited the fort. Today some of the concrete infrastructure from the war has been buried for preservation. (David Goss.)

Synonymous with the community of Mispec, this beach has been one of Saint John's recreation areas since 1967, although it is outside the city boundary. From 1947 until 1967, the beach was the responsibility of the St. John County government. The beach as a passive recreation area dates to the third quarter of the 19th century. Saint John residents spent the day travelling by horse-drawn buggy or taking special trips arranged by boat. In 1898, the tug *Storm King* ran a two-day excursion to the beach so visitors could view the pulp mill then under construction. In 1947, the county council purchased the former navy signals building at Mispec beach. It was converted into a canteen, dance floor, bathing house, and coat check rooms. An expanded parking lot and a children's play area with swings completed the facility. (Above, HR12876; below, HR12859.)

Seven

Sports, Horses, and Amusements

Saint John East has had, and still has, its share of recreational amenities. Here is one of the earliest, the Bicycle and Athletic Grounds on Rothesay Avenue at Marsh Creek. It was established privately by sportsmen long before it became de rigueur for cities to build such facilities. This photograph depicts the grounds in 1910; by 1916, it was replaced by the East End Ground across from Cooper's Corner. (HR11351.)

The War Vets team of the East Suburban League at the East End Grounds in the 1920s included Saint John's famous speedskater, Charlie Gorman (standing, fourth from the left). Gorman was offered a professional contract in 1925 with the New York Yankees farm team. He was coached at one point by Frank White, the famed Saint John candymaker whose peppermint recipe is still used by Ganongs to this day. The St. John team won 8 to 5 against the DAAA team. (New Brunswick Sports Hall of Fame.)

It was important for those serving in the military to keep in shape, and what would be more Canadian to do that than to play hockey? This 8th Anti-Aircraft Battery team of the East End Barracks were City Champions. There were a number of natural outdoor ice surfaces nearby in the bogs behind Mary Ann's Hill, on lands where the match factory stored their lumber for drying. (HR1156.)

The earliest horse races were held on the mudflats on Courtenay Bay. Moosepath Driving Park at Coldbrook opened August 23, 1871, the day the famed Paris and Renforth crew race was held on the Kennebecasis. David Lynch is one of these drivers at Moosepath around 1890. In 1930, the Exhibition Association opened Coldbrook Park off Golden Grove Road. Racing was a year-round event but was most popular during Exhibition Week. (HR6732.)

In June 1938, the Robbins Brothers Circus came to the East End Grounds and did a parade and three shows. They visited the children at the TB hospital and the Protestant and Roman Catholic Orphanages. Free tickets were given to the boys of the Industrial Home. In this image are, from left to right, (first row) the Ross Brothers Trio of acrobatic clowns—unidentified, Happy Kellums, and Van Wells, the comic cop; (second row) Gordie Crockett and newspaper reporter Charles Lynch. (HR6810.)

The Simonds Rink on McAllister Drive was built to mark Canada's Centennial in 1967. Sonny McDonald managed it for most of the four decades it stood. Though not fancy, it was beloved by East Saint John skaters and dubbed by some as the "Simonds Ice Palace." In summer, events now held at Harbour Station, like the home show and the boat show, were staged there, along with car shows, circuses, revivals, and rock shows. In August, it was used during the ANE for stage shows with international performers. The pool was added to Simonds High when it was built in 1970. It was the first joint financing effort between the city and the school board. Until the downtown Aquatic Centre opened in 1983, most Saint Johners learned to swim at this pool. (David Goss.)

Moosepath Driving Park was established north of Marsh Road with proximity to the newly built rail line, an important consideration in the site selection. By the 1930s, it had fallen on hard times. The new Coldbrook Park oval, on land later purchased by the Exhibition Association for $75,000 from the Roman Catholic diocese, is seen at the top. Between the two ovals, Marsh Creek meanders through the fields and Rothesay Avenue runs straight towards its termination at Torryburn. (HR-Kent.)

When the exhibition began again in 1954, the entertainers did outdoor shows in front of the huge racetrack grandstand that had been constructed in 1930 when Coldbrook Park opened. It could seat 4,000 spectators, who enjoyed novelty acts, such as the horse show in this photograph, one of a series that showed trampoline and high-wire acts, trick dogs, acrobatic novelties, clowns at play, and music from the local band. (HR9758.)

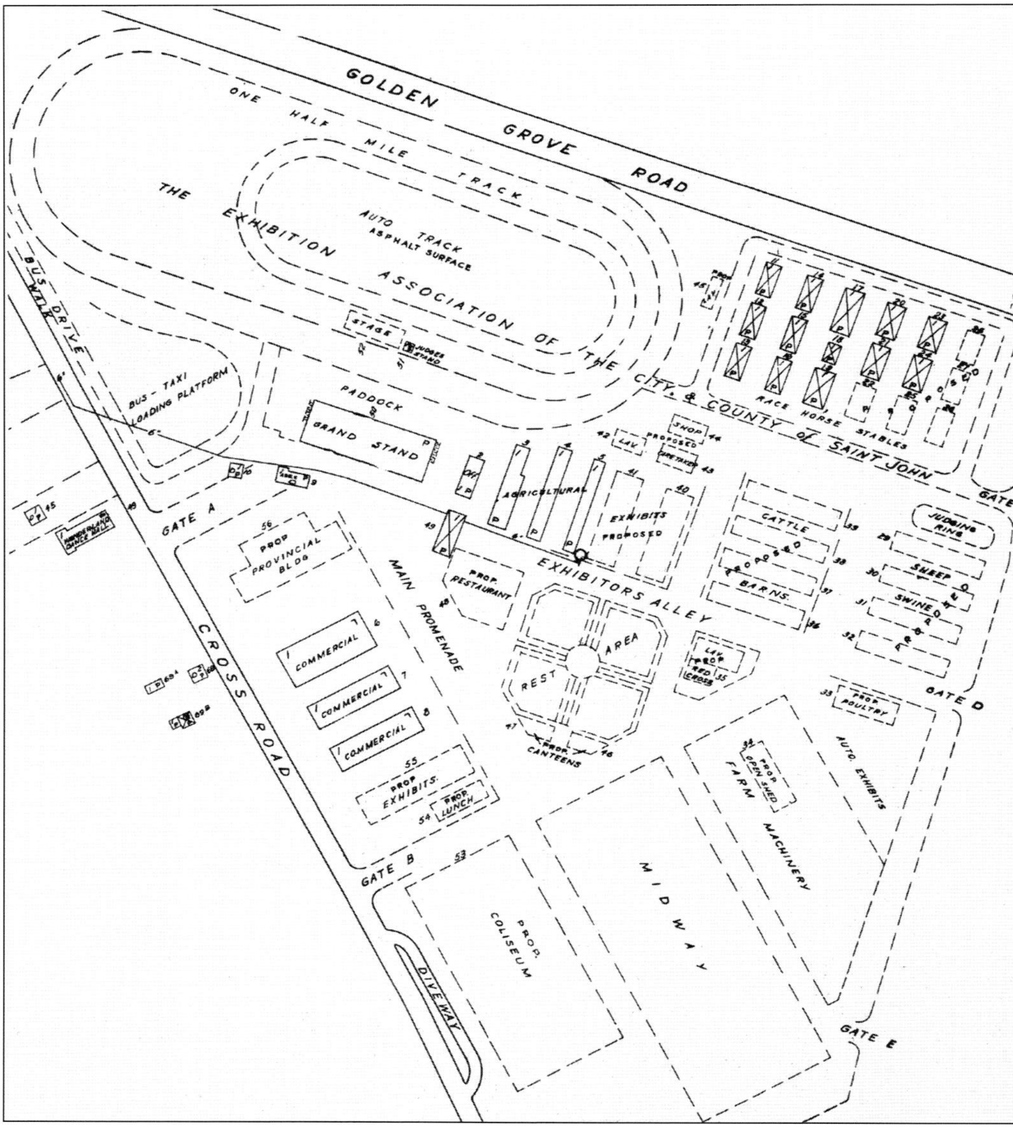

This 1957 overview of the Exhibition Grounds shows the hopes and dreams of the Exhibition Association of the City and County of Saint John. This group was formed in 1889 and, until 1938, held an annual fall exhibition at the Barrack Green in the South End. Exhibitions were cancelled during the war years, and it was not until 1954 that they resumed. The Atlantic National Exhibition (ANE) moved to Coldbrook Park, and over the next decade and a half, as much of what was planned in 1957 was accomplished. Huge crowds, usually in the range of 100,000 for the week, attended the annual last-of-August week of fun. In 1957, McAllister Drive was called Cross Road. The proposed coliseum became the Simonds Rink (as noted on page 60).The horse racing oval at that time also had a half-mile car racetrack used for exciting stock car races for many years. (HR-Wright.)

These views show some of the staff working at the ANE. The ticket taker works for the Bill Lynch Hippodrome. Bill Lynch provided the amusement rides and sideshows for the annual ANE from 1954 until his death in 1988. The exhibition was essentially a family show, but the exotic dancer was part of the "For Adults Only" show. There is a long tradition of circus-like acts being frequent visitors to Saint John over the decades, many travelling from the Eastern United States and venturing into Canada via the Boston Boat. In the early days, performers travelled by horse and wagon; later they came by train; and today these acts arrive in specially designed vans. (Right, HR7511; below, HR9451.)

The Bill Lynch show brought the latest in rides to the ANE. Erma Wright, the author's mother, looks like she is about to enjoy a ride on the Rock 'N Roller in 1966. Over the years, the ANE has featured such rides as the Spider, the Trabant, the Bumper Cars, the Zipper, the Caterpillar, the Hurricane, and the Tip Top, and of course there were the sideshows and the games. (H.E. Wright.)

What is an exhibition or circus without a clown? This is Bob the Clown, representing CFBC Radio station, the city's leading station when this photograph was taken in the late 1950s. It is hard to say who is having the most fun—Bob or the two youngsters on the merry-go-round. (HR12011.)

Eight

We Stand on Guard

Camp Torryburn was a small campground used by the militia for their summer training camp. In 1864, it was used for a military review when some 1,400 soldiers, both British regulars and local militia, were reviewed before more than 3,000 civilians. In 1870, a proper rifle range was built and became known as the Drury Cove Range. The St. John Rifle Company is seen on the range on July 1, 1897, but after the militia were issued the Lee Enfield rifle, the range was deemed unsafe for modern firearms and closed. (HR10537.)

After Marsh Creek, at the right was the old East End ball field. In 1940, this was closed and the land leased to the military. They had already established temporary quarters for the 8th Anti-Aircraft Battery, which was tasked with providing antiaircraft defences against attacking Luftwaffe aircraft. As shown here in 1942, the camp was located behind the homes fronting on Thorne Avenue. After the war, the land was sold for commercial developments and Dominion Store and Canadian Tire located there. (HR1612.)

During home defence, life could become a bit tedious and boring for soldiers. In this case, these gunners of the 8th Anti-Aircraft Battery at the East End Grounds are starting the war on September 2, 1939, with an enthusiastic round of music, song, and drink. Ollie Cormier has the mouth organ. (HR1154.)

Capt. Freeland "Buzz" DeVenne of the 3rd Coast Brigade parades the gunners behind their band on Thorne Avenue across from the Church of England cemetery. The gunners of the 4th and 15th Batteries, along with the 1st Searchlight and 8th Anti-Aircraft Batteries, manned the harbour defences against attack by the German navy and air force. Later in the war, a reserve unit of this brigade was quartered at the East End Grounds. (HR1020.)

Driver Harold McKay is seen here with the ration truck at the East End Grounds. Since men from this battery were stationed at several locations—such as Fort Howe, the Slaughter House, and the dry dock—food had to be taken to these locations every few days. McKay, born in Ontario in 1919, joined the army in May 1942 at Saint John but shortly after was sent overseas. He was discharged in March 1946 in London, Ontario. (HR10989.)

The antiaircraft defences for the St. John Dry Dock in 1942 included this antiquated Vickers machine gun on an antiaircraft mounting. The four-man gun crew fed the belt of ammunition to the gun while a water tank kept the barrel from overheating. This gun pit was on the grounds of the Boys Industrial Home, and in the background is the East Saint John School. (HR11007.)

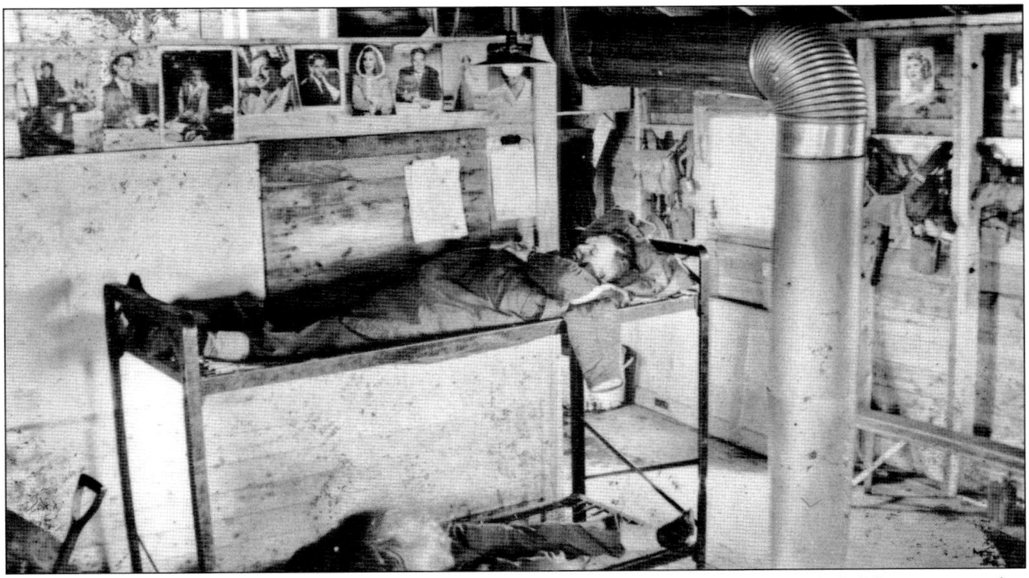

Harold McKay took this photograph at one of the 8th battery's outposts in 1942. He captioned it "Officer on Duty," which probably related to the man asleep on the top bunk. A closer examination reveals the pot-bellied stove to warm the entire building, a single hanging light bulb, the handle of a coal shovel, web equipment hanging on the walls, pinups, and one other soldier asleep on the bottom bunk. (HR10996.)

This anti-motor torpedo boat battery was located at the west end of the Courtenay Bay breakwater. In October 1939, gunners of the 4th Coast Battery, 3rd New Brunswick Coast Brigade placed an 18-pounder field gun at the end of the breakwater. In 1940, a large concrete gun gantry was constructed, camouflaged to look like a fishing shed. The Battery Observation Post was made to look like a lighthouse. The battery closed on September 1, 1944. (HR1665.)

When this photograph was taken in 1943 at the Slaughter House antiaircraft site in Loch Lomond, the chances of a German air attack on Saint John were greatly diminished. The 3.7-inch gun was in a sunken concrete gun pit surrounded by sand bags. A nearby magazine stored the ammunition and gunner quarters were located away from the gun. The gunners are still carrying out camouflage work to hide the gun position. In the background is St. Mary's cemetery on Loch Lomond Road. The Loch Lomond Mall was built across from the battery position, and recently the new Saint John transit garage was built to the left of this site. (Left, HR1674; below, HR1675.)

Gunner Tom Patrick from Hampton stands sentry in front of No. 3 gun at Fort Mispec. This battery was the major counter-bombardment fort in the harbour defence network for World War II. The 7.5-inch guns were to engage a German surface vessel on its approach up the Bay of Fundy. In July 1940, gunners of the 4th Battery, 3rd New Brunswick Coast Brigade, Royal Canadian Artillery had the guns ready for action. (HR1291.)

The three-gun battery at Fort Mispec consisted of 7.5-inch guns as shown here at No. 1 emplacement. There was also an observation post on a hill across the Red Head Road, as well as three magazines, a power plant, several barracks, and mess halls. The camouflage scheme was to make the fort resemble a fishing village. After the war, many of the wooden buildings were sold and converted to homes. (HR1643.)

The gun crews at Fort Mispec spent the war keeping a watchful eye for the enemy. At the end of the war, gunners took comfort in knowing that their presence prevented the Germans from attacking. Although not known until after the war, Saint John was visited by the dreaded U-boat. In 1942, U-boats U-553 and U-213 entered the Bay of Fundy; one laid off Partridge Island for six nights, and the other landed a spy at St. Martins. (HR1266.)

After the war, the Canadian Legion established the Simonds Branch no. 53 in the McAvity's Castle next to the dry dock on Bayside Drive. Later they changed their name to the Jervis Bay Branch to commemorate the gallant action of HMS *Jervis Bay*, which had her final outfitting done at the dry dock two months before her final voyage. The Jervis Bay Legion recently relocated to Grandview Avenue in 2010. (HR10639.)

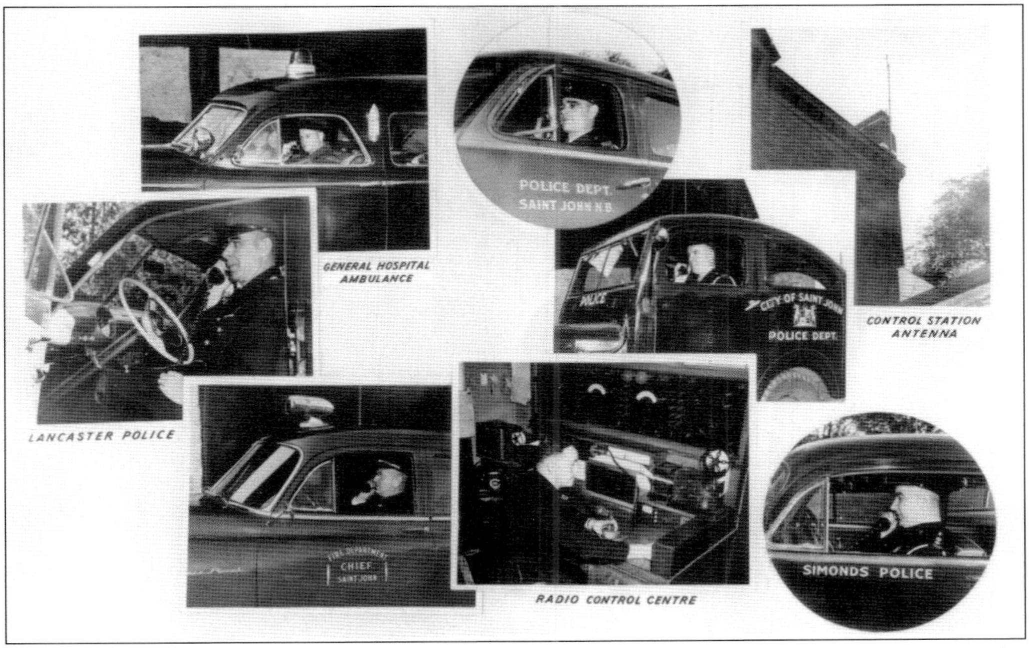

Photographs of the Simonds Police Department are very rare. This 1950 collage shows the municipal radio system for the police, fire, and ambulance services for the County of Saint John. At the bottom right, an unidentified Simonds officer uses the radio telephone. Though small in numbers, officers from the parish of Simonds solved one of the areas most heinous crimes, the 1955 Clifford Edward Ayles robbery and murder at the TB hospital. (HR10669.)

East Saint John had both paid and volunteer firefighters prior to amalgamation with Saint John in 1967. Companies like McAvity's, the dry dock, and the Irving Oil Refinery had their own fire services. In June 1977, fire destroyed the Peterson Variety Store in the Morland Trailer Park off Rothesay Avenue. (HR8273.)

On June 20, 1922, No. 1 Company of the Saint John Salvage Corps and Fire Police went to the Log Cabin Fishing Club at Loch Lomond to celebrate their 40th anniversary. They are, from left to right, (first row) Thomas Tonge, W. J. Currie, Dr. L. A. Langstroth, C. Robinson, and Fred Doig; (second row) P. Carson and W. E. Campbell. East Saint John did not have a Salvage Corps and Fire Police organization. (HR8316.)

In the mid-1950s, the Simonds Fire Department had at least two vehicles. One was the ladder truck shown here and the other a pumper still inside the Courtenay Avenue station. The ladder truck had a crew of four, as evidenced by the four helmets on the side of the vehicle. Fire stations have always been popular attractions for visitors, as shown by the family of three in front of the department's truck. (HR7892.)

In October 1955, Simonds fire chief Raymond H. Woodruff had this portrait taken to record his role in the history of the Simonds Fire Department. He was one of a few chiefs of this department. After amalgamation with the Saint John Fire Department in 1967, the men of the Simonds department were absorbed into the larger municipal fire service. (HR7427.)

The fear of every home owner is fire. On Sunday evening, May 22, 1977, this three-storey home on Golden Grove Road was destroyed, leaving 12 people homeless. The building, owned by Gerald Legassie, was formerly known as the Eaton House and was located across from Superior Concrete Products Ltd. To fight the fire, the 14 firefighters had to pump water from a nearby brook. (HR2617.)

For the parishioners of St. Joachim's Church at Silver Falls, on the Loch Lomond Road, New Year's Day 1977 was not a day to celebrate. It took firefighters 6 hours and 33 minutes to extinguish the fire that destroyed the rear portion and damaged the main section of their century-old church. Three pump companies, four tankers, an aerial truck, and the rescue unit fought the blaze. A new church was built on the site and continues to serve the community to this day. (Above, HR8243; below, HR8244.)

On August 28, 1974, the employees of Crosby's Molasses on Rothesay Avenue were saddened when fire destroyed part of the company plant. One of the hazards for firefighters with commercial properties is the unknown: were these barrels full of syrup, a food product, or a chemical used in the cleaning of plant equipment? In this case, there were no hazardous materials to deal with. (HR8280.)

After the August 3, 1977, fire at Deluxe French Fries at 471 Rothesay Avenue, it was the job of the fire inspectors to examine the interior to determine the cause of the fire. Sometimes it was be obvious, such as with a grease fire, or it could be a hidden electrical problem. Fire inspectors, after years of service as firefighters, take specialized training to do a forensic analysis of a fire scene. (HR2604.)

Firefighter Arnold Buck performs one of the delightful duties of a firefighter by showing off the station equipment to young visitors. Arnold joined the Saint John Fire Department in 1959. He served in several stations, including No. 4 on Courtenay Avenue and later No. 2 on Loch Lomond Road. After 32 years of service, Captain Buck retired as the officer in charge of No. 2 station in 1991. (HR9563.)

Nine

The Commercial and Industrial East

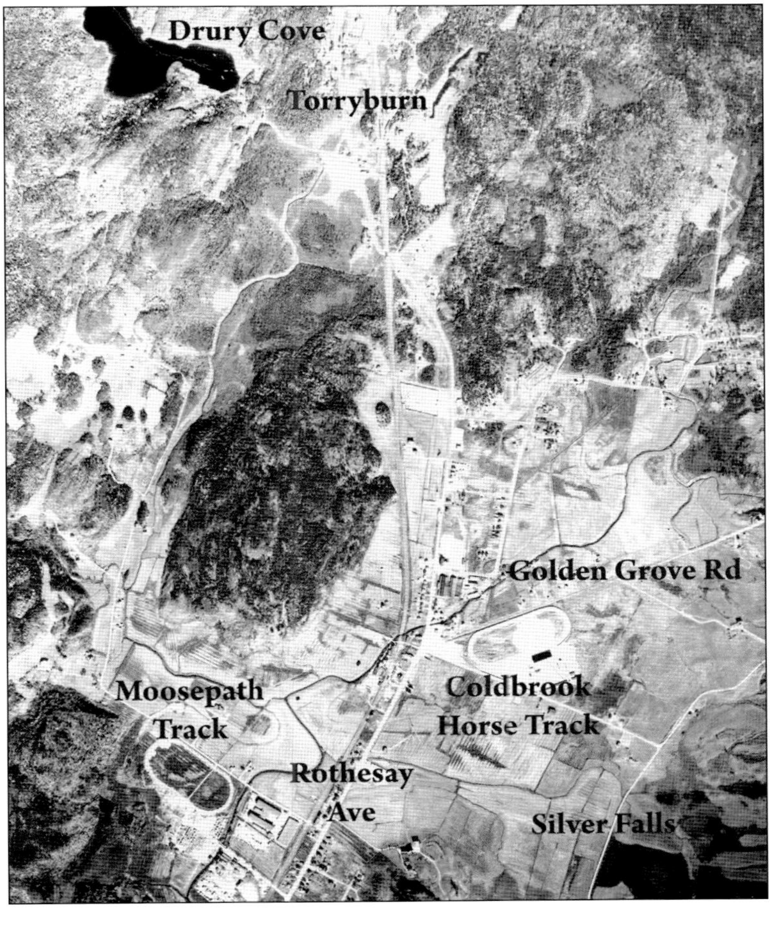

This mid-1950s aerial shows Rothesay Avenue and neighbourhood from a perspective that few get to see. Both the Moosepath and Coldbrook racing ovals are visible. The military buildings next to Moosepath are now part of Strescon on Rothesay Avenue. The housing development at Forest Hills has not yet begun, and there are still a few houses in Glen Falls. The CHSJ television tower and building are just to the left of the word Coldbrook. CHSJ-TV went on the air in 1954. (HR11325.)

This shows the only entrance into East Saint John before the Courtenay Bay Causeway was built in the mid-1960s. Many folks remember the 1954 rescue of Fred J. Esson from the McAvity smokestack. He got stuck at the top and a helicopter from Greenwood came to his rescue. The rescue was shown on CHSJ television that night, the first time a same-day news story was shown on television in North America. (HR4455.)

A dapper-looking Wilfred Harley is shown at the intersection of Russell Street and Rothesay Avenue in 1923. This area had quite a reputation in the 1880s. There was a house called the Long Boat whose inmates were known to give a lot of trouble to the police, being the residents of a scene of lively fights. In 2010, much of Russell Street was redeveloped for the One Mile House Interchange. (HR9818.)

This view from Coopers Corner reveals a lot about the entrance to the East End from the Marsh Creek Bridge. The Haymarket Square Irving, Bank of Montreal, and the Aberdeen School are visible. Atop Vinegar Hill is the old General Hospital before the 1959 addition. The Imperial Esso station on the east side of the Marsh Creek Bridge would soon be demolished for the construction of the Dominion Store. This picture was taken from the Texaco station. (HR6660.)

The west end of Rothesay Avenue had several new and used car lots as well as automobile garages. Dykeman and Lawson Motors are shown, as is Central Equipment and the McAvity smokestack. The two policemen and small crowd at the right reveal the true reason behind why this photograph was taken. The car at the left has crashed into the corner of the building, knocking over one of the used car lot signs. (HR3644.)

In the late 1940s and 1950s, Saint John Motors was the Dodge DeSoto dealer in the city. It was also a British American gas and service station, a combination of sales and service not found with automobile dealers today. The DeSoto was made between 1928 and 1961. The stockroom and repair shop were destroyed by fire in December 1951, which damaged over 60 new and privately owned cars. (HR9018.)

Ellis Motors, pictured across from the McAvity plant in 1950, offered 1949 Ford Monarchs for sale. Shortly thereafter, the company suffered a fire. Wilson's Sales and Service relocated here from Waterloo Street and reopened in December 1952. Brett Motors is the car dealership occupying the building now. In front of the fender service garage is an International panel ambulance, and to the right of the telephone pole is a 1948 Ford half-ton. (HR4148.)

Lorenzo G. Crosby started his company in 1879 at Yarmouth, Nova Scotia, and soon after began trade with the West Indies, importing puncheons filled with that sweet and tasty "liquid gold" known today as fancy molasses. In 1897, he moved his business to Saint John and, 14 years later, relocated to the Great Marsh Road, the present location (above). Delivery methods have changed over the years. No longer are horses and wagons used to transport the puncheons of molasses. After 123 years in business, Crosby today utilizes the latest in technology in both the production and delivery of its molasses, drink flavour crystals, pancake mix, and marshmallow fluff throughout Canada, the United States, and to some overseas locations. (Above, HR13164; below, Crosby Molasses Ltd.)

Rothesay Avenue was the food centre from the 1950s through the 1970s. In May 1971, Theodore Likourgiotis, Mike Feggos, and George Flogeras, all recent Greek immigrants, opened the Mediterranean Restaurant. The first Saint John McDonalds opened nearby in 1973–1974. Two well known drive-ins along the avenue in the 1950s and 1960s were the Roll 'N Shake and the Dog 'N Suds. The Flame, at the far end of Rothesay Avenue, was a popular eatery from 1959 until the early 1980s. (Don Collins.)

Rothesay Avenue saw many kinds of repair services over the years, but airplane repair was definitely not one of them. On December 31, 1941, this Avro Anson Mk. 1 did a nose landing in Coldbrook. The pilot may have been Leo Cook. The records for this Anson, No. 6724, do not list this accident. The aircraft was from the air base at Pennfield Ridge. No Ansons were stationed in Saint John during the war. (David Goss.)

Hilda and Ray Holland were the first operators of their grill and motel at the corner of Holland Street and Rothesay Avenue in the 1950s and 1960s. Terry (Parlee) Munn had her first job there as a 12-year-old. Her first task was to peel potatoes, something she had never done before. Parlee used the wrong side of the paring knife, for which she received some gentle teasing. When she told her dad, Charlie, he replied, "Any fool can do it the other way." (HR9644.)

Jeffrey "Sonny" Collins was the owner of the Glen Falls Motel and Restaurant when this postcard was made in 1962. There were several area motels, including the Sandman and the Wandalyn. Automobile visitors wanted accommodation cheaper than the uptown hotels, such as the Admiral Beatty and the Royal. (Don Collins.)

Sometimes a historic photograph reveals more than just the obvious. This image, taken in the 1950s near the corner of Broadway Avenue where Sterling Apples is located, shows many things. The most obvious is the large sign for Clarence Brown's Speedway Garage selling White Rose gasoline. Other signs are for Sussex beverages, "Lunches" and, in the background, an appliance store. (HR7005.)

The Brodersen Farm, 492 Rothesay Avenue, is pictured here in the 1930s. This farm was located just a short distance past the Fernhill Cemetery entrance, near where the Mercedes-Benz car dealership is today. There were two barns on the property, and the owner was Tommy Hayes. He rented the second floor flat to the Brodersens, with an option to buy. Hayes had already rented the first floor to the McKinney family, who had three children—Clifford, Viola, and a baby whose name is not known. (Val Ward.)

Terkild Brodersen, a Danish citizen, was conscripted in the German army during World War I. He is shown here tending to his garden during World War II. The buildings in the background are for the military police. During this war, Terkild and his German wife, Hertha, may have been under surveillance as possible German spies. A letter to the editor of the Saint John newspaper decried the harassment of foreigners as possible spies. Gertrude Berteit, sister of Hertha Brodersen, is also tending the garden on the 5-acre farm on Rothesay Avenue. The wooded area in the background is part of Fernhill Cemetery. Her nephew Thor eventually set up his sign-making shop, Neon and Plastic Signs Ltd., nearby, spending more than 50 years in the sign making business. (Val Ward.)

Joseph E. Arrowsmith started his St. John Spring Works on Thorne Avenue in 1919, shortly after returning from the Great War. He retired in 1945 and died two years later. The Spring Works is still in the Arrowsmith family and offers a wide range of services for the transportation industry—rustproofing, truck repair and service, shock absorbers, and as their motto states, "If It's A Spring, Give Us A Ring." (HR6136.)

This 1931 comic postcard for Fundy gasoline was sent to Arthur T. Dodge in Greenwich, Kings County, Nova Scotia. It also contained a coupon for "Graigrene Lubricant," which "neither freezes nor channels," as well as a brochure for Loyal Motor Oil, of the Canadian Independent Oil Ltd., East Saint John. This oil company was owned by Allan G. McAvity, who resided in the family castle near the dry dock and later served as a Member of Parliament. (HR-75-2-3-4.)

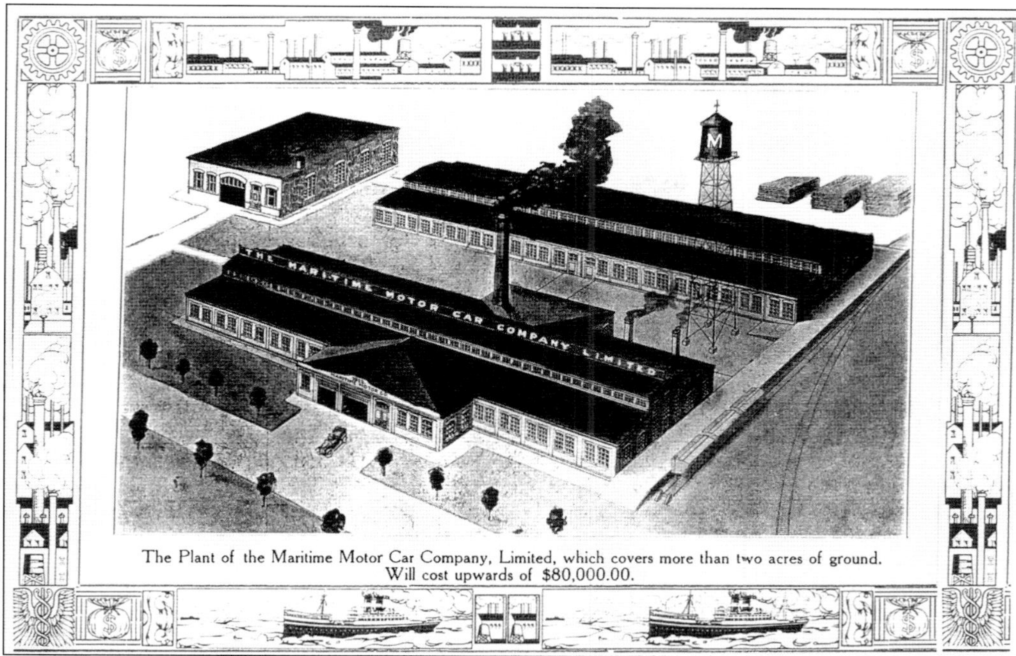

The Plant of the Maritime Motor Car Company, Limited, which covers more than two acres of ground. Will cost upwards of $80,000.00.

In 1912, J. A. Pugsley built his Maritime Motor Company plant in Glen Falls. Associated with the Ford Motor Company, the most famous car built here was the Singer Six. Pugsley also owned the Coldbrook Realty and Development Company, which promoted "land where you can grow your own vegetables, have a little garden, and plenty of God's fresh air for your wife and family." In the 1920s, Ford cars were sold here, and later it was the D. F. Brown box factory. (HR-Wright.)

The Maritime Singer Six was the first automobile to be assembled in Saint John. It had a short production life, and only four to five cars were assembled. To show the versatility of this car, a 1913 demonstration drive took place between Saint John and Halifax. It took 156 hours to make the journey, spending more time shovelling snow than driving. (David Goss.)

In 1963, East Saint John's first mall, the Kwik-Pik, opened in the former box company building on Brown Street. There were 14 stores inside the building, offering everything from appliances, sporting goods, and hardware to a 14-stool snack bar, clothing, beauty aids, tobacco, and fresh vegetables. The first manager was Bill Delay, who was quick to point out to wary shoppers that the mall had a complete air-conditioning system for both summer and winter use. (HR-Wright.)

This is F. F. Farren's Texaco service station at Coopers Corner, towards the end of the 1940s. This image reveals much of what early full-service stations offered. There was the uniformed attendant who filled the gas tank and washed drivers' windshields. A car could be greased, lubricated, and washed, and there was a bay just for work on tires and batteries. There was also a public washroom and a tire pump. Next to the station was Robert's Grill. (HR9017.)

At the left of this pre-1955 view of Thorne Avenue is one of the few remaining residential houses. The International Harvester building is now Chandler Sales. Just beyond is the Esso Station, later a Tim Hortons. Across the street is a gas sign for Superline. In the foreground, a new foundation has been laid for what is now a paint store. Beyond that is an empty lot, which by 1955 became the site of the Canada Packers plant. (HR9019.)

This is a photograph of Alick Taylor's store taken early in World War II. Many mistakenly refer to this as Kanes Corner, which was across the street. Taylor was quite involved with the community. He proposed amalgamation with Saint John in 1935 so Simonds could have access to the city's sewerage system. In the 1970s, this building was home to Splane's Sporting Goods. The brick building behind Taylor's was the old Eddy match factory. (H. E. Wright.)

Charlie Parlee is on the steps of this store at 91 Russell Street in 1936. Born in 1916, Charlie had a few occupations, including driving a meat truck during the Depression. He eventually became a Power Mechanic at the Irving Pulp Mill. Charlie built his home on Broadway Avenue in Glen Falls, which he later sold to Doug Defazio for his body shop. (Terry Munn.)

The Bricklin SV-1 was a gull-wing sports car assembled in the Grandview Avenue Industrial Park from 1974 to 1976. The designer of the car was Herb Grasse, the man behind TV's original Batmobile. Nicholas Osgood, a tool and die maker from England, worked there from 1975 until the factory closed. He remembers, "Being only a small shop with about 15 men we often had our pay 'delayed' a week or two due to Bricklins current condition." Only 2,854 cars were built before the company went into receivership. (HR13084.)

In 1960, K. C. Irving built his oil refinery at Silver Falls (above). One of the smartest marketing moves was the location of six storage tanks facing Loch Lomond Road, each painted with one letter of the name Irving. Although a little difficult to see in the photograph below, these letters were clearly visible in person, even at night. Irving initially had a partner, Chevron Oil, but bought out Chevron's share in the late 1980s. Environmental technology in the early decades of the refinery's life left a lot to be desired for the nearby residents of Champlain Heights. Over the past two decades, the refinery has invested hundreds of millions of dollars in new technology, making this one of the most efficient in Canada. The refinery now produces some of the lowest-emission petroleum in North America. The Silver Falls marsh has been rehabilitated by Ducks Unlimited. (Above, HR13054; below, HR7114.)

Roy Milne is pictured here in the yard of International Harvester on Thorne Avenue. In later years, he worked at the new Bayview International Trucks on McAllister Drive. Roy was born in 1925 and died in the late 1980s. When he started with International, he was the company accountant. He later became the comptroller for Bayview. For many years, Roy owned and lived in the former Robert Jardine house, Woodside, on the Marsh Road. (Pam Milne-Vincent.)

The Old Manor House, built about 1815 for James Cudlip of the Royal Navy, was a well-known inn and dining and dance hall. Destroyed by fire in 1920, it sat opposite St. Anne's Church on Simpson Drive. There were other dance hall locations in the Glen. In 1920, the children of the Glen Falls Summer Colony gave a concert in the O'Hara pavilion. In 1926, the Glen Falls Community Club held a social evening for 20 couples in their clubhouse. The area's first tavern was the Frog Pond, near the present site of the Three Mile. (Don Collins.)

Walter Pedersen, the florist, had his retail shop in the City Market building. He specialized in bridal bouquets, funeral designs, banquet, church, and wedding decorations. In 1913, he built his greenhouse in Glen Falls behind the Manor House on 10 acres of land purchased from the Coldbrook Realty and Improvement Company. The greenhouse had 50,000 square feet of glass. His brother Kris also had a greenhouse on Sandy Point Road. (HR12998.)

In August 1929, Lawrence Young of Montreal spent a two-week vacation in Saint John. A legacy of that trip is an amazing photograph album documenting two weeks in the life of the city. Young visited the Fundy Fox Farm on Bayside Drive, an enterprise in which it is believed Allan G. McAvity also had part ownership. (HR3248.)

Another place that Lawrence Young visited was the Dominion Fish Hatchery near Blind Man's Lake and the "Res." This 1929 photograph shows the trout runway. For most of its history, the hatchery spawned trout for stocking lakes in southern New Brunswick. The last fish type at the hatchery before it closed was the sturgeon. (HR3259.)

This 1960s aerial view shows the fish hatchery at the lower end of the Res on Loch Lomond Road. Blind Mans Lake and Loch Lomond Road are at the left. Hickey Road is at the right of the Res and shows the intersection with Grandview Avenue at the centre right. The "Res" was the reservoir for the city's Loch Lomond water supply. (HR4713.)

This image has been doctored, probably for a 1930s newspaper advertisement. It shows the Brookville Manufacturing plant, the St. John Lime Company, and the Adams Lime Works, in Brookville. The menacing sky has been added, as has been the steam train. The car in the foreground is part of the original photograph. Lime is still quarried in this same area today. (HR9433.)

This 1937 view of the International Fertilizer plant off Bayside Drive shows much about this area of the east. At the left are the fuel storage tanks of Irving Oil. At the top left is the old alms or poorhouse or, as the city fathers preferred it to be called, the Municipal Home. The dry dock is at the right. Eventually all of this property became part of the dry dock. (HR6115.)

A lot has changed since this 1969 view was taken. It shows the Courtenay Bay power plant in the foreground and, to its left, the former McMillan paper plant, now owned by Irving. Behind the power plant is the East Saint John hospital, and behind that is the Willet Fruit Company building. Around the dry dock property can still be seen a few private homes and some of the World War II buildings. (HR4780.)

Behind Marsh Creek, a city transit bus sits outside the Canadian National Railway (CNR) roundhouse. The Irving-owned bus company moved here after a disastrous fire destroyed their garage off Winter Street. The advertisement for the Coldbrook Iron Works, located off the Golden Grove Road, shows that this company made railway spikes and probably other rail items. (David Goss.)

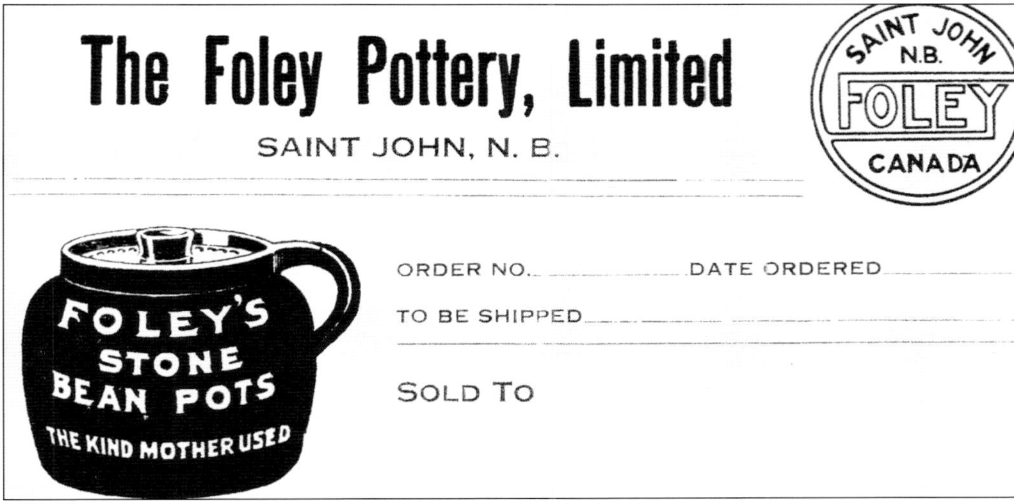

The Foley Pottery, Limited

SAINT JOHN, N. B.

SAINT JOHN N.B. FOLEY CANADA

FOLEY'S STONE BEAN POTS THE KIND MOTHER USED

ORDER NO. DATE ORDERED

TO BE SHIPPED

SOLD TO

This bill head for a bean crock reveals only one of the hundreds of their products. Foley's was one of the largest employers in the area before the opening of both the McAvity Foundry and the dry dock. In 1864, Joseph White bought William Warnick pottery near the corner of Mount Pleasant Avenue East and Bayside Drive. In 1880, this became Poole and Foley Pottery. In 1885, the plant burned and relocated to Loch Lomond Road. (HR-Wright.)

This is the Foley plant off Loch Lomond Road in 1898. The company went through many name changes. In 1900, it was the James W. Foley Company and, in 1921, Foley Pottery Ltd. In 1946, it relocated to its original spot on Mount Pleasant Avenue East and became Canuck Pottery. (HR10395.)

Foley Pottery staff pose in 1902. They are, from left to right, (first row) Sam Foley, Joe McCormack, Jimmy Foley, four unidentified, Dave Ramsey, and James Foley (father of Sam and Jimmy); (second row) Ike Fawcett, unidentified, Blunt Hanlin, Charlie Gordon, Bob Nelson, unidentified, Jack Walsh, and Fred and Margaret Foley. The following men are also in the photograph, but it is not known exactly who they are: Frank Hicks, Bill Hayes, Fred Hayter, Jack Pinny, and Cliff Gordon. (HR10381.)

Fire destroyed the Foley plant in December 1944. F. D. Foley discovered the fire at 6:45 a.m. as he was on his way to work. It began in the rear of the plant, called the main shop. In addition to the Simonds Fire Department, a pumper from uptown was also dispatched, allowing four hoses to be used on the blaze. By 7:30 a.m., the firefighters, under Chief J. H. MacKenzie, succeeded in saving the front of the building, the warehouse, from the flames. By 9:30 a.m., the fire was under control. Saved from the blaze were the company records, one kiln of pottery already fired, and the clay shed. Another fire, in 1964, destroyed the new plant on Bayside Drive, so Canuck pottery relocated to Quebec. (Right, HR10389; below, HR-Foley.)

Margaret Foley is pictured here in a Saxon Runabout with 1916 license no. 4667. The 2-seat Runabout was the first car made by the Saxon Motor Car Company of Detroit. It had electric lighting, a 2-speed transmission, and a 6-cylinder engine. Margaret married Alfred Eckebrecht in June 1918. (HR10838.)

Fen Foley was the last of his family to ply the pottery trade in Saint John. After Canuck moved to Quebec, Fen operated a small studio from his home on Bayside Drive. He spent most of his time giving classes in pottery making. In 1969, Diane Latta, along with her father, R. K. Latta, visited Fen. She made one piece that she has kept to this day. (HR10401.)

McAvity's started as a hardware dealer in 1834. In 1863, they began to manufacture goods in brass and iron along Water Street in the uptown and, in 1916, began to construct their large foundry on Rothesay Avenue. The foundation work, with manpower and horsepower, not machinery, is seen in the foreground; Rothesay Avenue crosses mid-photograph, and the CN Rail line, with a Canadian Pacific Railway (CPR) steam engine at work, is at the top of the image. (HR4909.)

McAvity's was built on a marshy, triangular 30 acres of the Gilbert estate between Russell Sreet and Marsh and Westmorland Roads. Construction started in April and finished in August 1916. The firm had considered centralizing their business, and when they received a contract from American interests to build munitions, it became possible (also upon receiving tax concessions from the city) to build the 81-foot-by-410-foot plant. (HR4905.)

The McAvity plant was designed by Lockwood, Green, and Company of Montreal, with construction overseen by local architect F. Neil Brodie. Contractors were Grant and Thorne of Saint John. It was built of reinforced concrete with hard pine framing. The sawtooth skylights provided lots of light to the interior, which had 16-foot ceilings throughout. This photograph was taken by Capt. C. S. Kent of the Saint John Flying Club. (HR-Kent.)

The plant stretched along Rothesay Avenue for over 400 feet and dominated all other structures in the area. The western end was office space, the centre portion the machine shop, and the eastern end was designed with an open concept and could be quickly expanded as needed. The plant had its own powerhouse with a 152-foot chimney. Fred Esson had to be rescued from the top in 1954. (HR6119.)

On its 100th anniversary on May 19, 1934, McAvity's had foundry branches in Montreal, Toronto, and Winnipeg. Products included bronze, iron, and steel valves; pipe and pipe fittings; plumbing fixtures; boilers and radiators; acid resisting bronze and chrome nickel steel; railway specialities; marine accessories; and its best known product, found in cities from coast to coast, fire hydrants. The company ceased operations in Saint John in 1965. (HR7160.)

Unknown at the time was that the American military secretly provided funding for the construction of the McAvity Foundry in order to produce artillery shells for their army. Shown here, a worker is using a large drill press for Operation No. 2, the drilling of the nose cone for the 9.2-inch shell. In various places around him, the worker has chalked off the number of shells he has drilled. (HR7169.)

In Operation No. 3, the process is called the "rough turn body," and the shell is on a lathe in which the worker is roughly shaping the diameter of the shell. Over the lathe there are two hoses spraying water on the shell. At the right, a female coworker is using callipers to measure the shell's size. This and the other shell production photographs were taken in 1918 by Isaac Erb. (HR7171.)

There were at least 28 different stages in the production of the 9.2-inch shells. This is Operation No. 28, the varnishing of the shell prior to shipment. These shells would have weighed over 200 pounds, and at the left four men have dollies that were used to move the finished shells one at a time to the shipping department, where they were loaded onto railcars for shipment to the United States. (HR7194.)

Production during the war years was so extensive that storage was spread to the outlying yards. These are the rough 9.2-inch shells before they went into the foundry. There is good use of the plant's exterior walls to advertise their many products. At its highest point of employment, 2,500 men, women, and boys worked in the plant; 400 remained when the plant's end came in the 1960s. (HR7199.)

Bookkeeper H. L. Treat's employee record book notes April 15, 1918, "this is the first time we have used female help." He makes negative comments like "quick tempered," "too loud and mouthy," and positive comments like "learned quickly" and "worked diligently." At right, May Leard (far left), a 23-year-old spindle worker, is pictured on a 15-minute break. Treat described her as "medium height and build, very quiet girl, minded her own business at all times." (HR5834.)

Paperwork is a big part of any operation with supplies to be procured, invoices to be sent out, and payrolls to be computed. McAvity's had many 25- and 50-year men among the staff who would say, if asked, "We work with the boss, not for him." George Pottle, pictured below, said that office staff required to visit the main plant found it to be a noisy, dusty, and hot environment compared to their work area. (HR7207.)

Draftsman George Pottle lived on Thorne Avenue, not more than a two-minute walk from the McAvity plant where he worked one summer while a student studying drafting at vocational school. In 1948, he was hired by H. Emms for full-time drafting work at McAvity's. He stayed 11 years, leaving in 1959 when he began to hear rumours that Crane was going to buy McAvity's and close it out. (HR11826.)

This 1911 Norton Griffiths' plan for Courtenay Bay does not reveal the dark side to the beginnings of this shipyard. A 1913 New York court case revealed a $25,000 payment to Torontonian Vivian Bartram to keep open the alleged Courtenay Bay contract, when in fact there was no contract. There were two Canadians and three Americans involved in the scheme to make millions of dollars on the contract, which they would be guaranteed to receive. The Honorable William Pugsley of Saint John was also implicated. (HR9713.)

Construction began in 1912 and continued until 1916 under the Norton Griffiths Company. Wartime restrictions on nonessential war work led to construction being halted. Work began again in 1918 under James Playfair and the Saint John Dry Dock and Shipbuilding Company Ltd. The outer dock was 650 feet, the inner dock 500 feet, and the width of the dock was 125 feet. (HR4294.)

The owners of the dry dock were James Playfair, a prominent mill and shipping owner in Ontario, from 1918 to 1934; Frank M. Ross, later a lieutenant governor of British Columbia and father-in-law of Prime Minister John Turner, from 1934 to 1945; Charles N. Wilson, owner of the Saint John Tug Boat Company and J. Splane Sporting Goods, from 1945 to 1960; and K. C. Irving and family, from 1960 until the yard closed in 2003. (HR3736.)

Shipbuilding, even with the most up-to-date safety practices, is a dangerous occupation. Accidents did happen, and sadly, over the years many employees were injured and some were killed. Among those killed on the job were Italian construction worker James Frisco, who died January 1915; engineer James T. Duke, in May 1919; and shipyard workers Andrew Ellis, March 1933; Sam Dunlavy, January 1941; and Gordon Marks, who died in April 1944. (Anita Grearson.)

To mark the beginning of construction on July 11, 1912, Norton Griffiths hosted a garden party at the Tenby Cottage, summer home of W. F. Burditt. Guests, including local business leaders and federal members of Parliament and the legislature, were received by Mrs. Laura Woods, wife of the lieutenant governor, and Mrs. Lucy Burditt. The Cambridge City Band provided music. A solid silver wheelbarrow was presented to the Honourable Mr. White, and Norton Griffiths, MP, presented a solid silver shield for the motorboat race celebrating the start of construction. (HR4294.)

The dry dock opened in October 1923. Its first customer was the Norwegian steamer *Kongshaven*. En route to Saint John to load potatoes for Havana, Cuba, the ship was badly damaged when it ran aground on Briar Island the week before. After the ship entered the dock, the shipyard was declared open for business. Permanent repairs were not made to the *Kongshaven*, as it was sold at auction from North Market Wharf two weeks later. (Anita Grearson.)

Initially the dry dock had two cranes, a blacksmith shop, fabrication shop, and a machine shop. There was also a marine railway dock system and its own fleet of tugs, including the *Ocean Eagle*, the *Gopher*, *Florence*, *J. H. Hackett*, *Margaret A. Hackett*, the *Katherine K.*, and the *Ballindalloch*. These were stationed at Saint John, Quebec City, Halifax, and Sydney, Nova Scotia. There was also the hopper *Foremost 17* and the dredge *Leconfield*. (HR-Kent.)

The M.V. *Kipawo* was the first ship built at the dry dock, being commissioned as a passenger and freight ferry in 1926 for the Dominion Atlantic Railway. Kipawo is a portmanteau of the first two letters of Kingsport, Parrsboro, and Wolfville. During World War II, *Kipawo* was used by the Royal Canadian Navy as an antisubmarine tender. It resumed ferry service afterwards until 1977. In 1982, the *Kipawo* returned to Parrsboro, where it is now used as the Ship's Company's performance centre. (HR-Boyer.)

In May 1928, the ship *Emperor of Montreal* arrived for repairs. Next to the *Emperor* is the harbour dredge *Leconfield*, owned by the dry dock. Both are in the inner dock. Previous to these vessels, the shipyard repaired both the *Emperor of Fredericton* and the *Emperor of Havana*. In the outer dock is the Canadian Pacific ship *Marloch*. Between 1923 and 1933, the shipyard repaired 532 vessels and built nine. (HR821.)

Jim Dixon joined the shipyard in July 1942 as an apprentice draftsman, making $33 a month. One of Jim's first jobs was to assist a senior apprentice who was to sketch and measure a ship. Jim, stating he was exactly 6-feet tall, became a human measuring stick, standing in front of or beside things while his coworker made measurement notes. Jim retired in March 1990 after 47 years and 9 months of service to the company. (Jim Dixon.)

During World War II, there were three Flower Class corvettes built at the shipyard. HMCS *Sackville*, today Canada's national naval memorial, is in the foreground, with HMCS *Moncton* in the background. There were also eight ships built for the Parks Line. There were six ships constructed for other lines, including the M.V. *Blue Cloud*, delivered to its new owners in May 1947. The *Blue Cloud* remained in the waters until 1999. (HR9449.)

After the Second World War, the shipyard built several smaller vessels for the Royal Canadian Navy. This shows the christening of the naval tug *St. Anthony*. Its sister tug was the *St. Charles*. Two minesweepers, the *Fundy* and *Miramichi*, were turned over to the French navy in 1954 as part of Canada's NATO contribution to the defence of Europe. (HR7399.)

It is hard to believe that the shipyard was ever this busy. There are 10 large vessels undergoing repairs shown in this August 20, 1947, photograph, in addition to a number of smaller vessels. Most of the buildings shown remained until the beginning of the frigate program in the 1980s, and a few are still standing at the closed shipyard today. (HR467.)

At the left is the 400-foot tidal dock built during World War II. In the main dock is HMCS *Magnificent*. Later HMCS *Bonaventure* was also refitted here. The *Maggie* made its first call in 1948 under command of Rothesay native Comdr. Gus R. Miles. On this first visit, the boat was in dock for 10 days for an inspection and some painting. It was again in the dry dock in 1949, 1950, 1953, and 1955. (Shearwater Museum.)

In December 1950, the *Maggie* was in the shipyard for repairs to the propellor. When the *Maggie*, and later the *Bonnie*, were in dry dock, most of the crew were given leave. The flight crews and aircraft were left behind at Shearwater. Instead of the men remaining aboard ship, they were housed in a tent city off Bayside Drive. Some of the Saint John men who were aboard the ship were Harold Hinch and Dell Lynch of Glen Falls, Neil Flicknell, Robert McCann, and Robert Horncastle. Leading Seaman Stewart Trenkowsky, an east side resident, also served aboard the *Maggie* on two occasions—1950–1951 and 1954–1956. In 1953 and 1954, he was on the naval overseer staff at the shipyard. (Above, Shearwater Museum; below, HR-Wright.)

The shipyard built more than just vessels. They provided steel for buildings and bridges. In 1948, the shipyard received the $3 million contract to built eight concrete cribs—107 feet long, 50 feet wide, and 50 feet high—to be used in building the new McLeod and Pettingill wharves off Water Street uptown. Once the concrete crib was floated into position, valves were opened to allow the crib to fill with water and sink into position. At low tide, there was 14 feet of concrete showing above water, which allowed the pier's superstructure to be built. (HR4690.)

Construction was a round-the-clock activity, rain or shine, summer or winter. Between 1972 and 1976, the Irving shipyard had a contract to built seven oil tankers for Esso, as shown here. They remained at sea until 2003. (HR10572.)

Between 1977 and 1978, the shipyard built four tankers for Shell Bermuda Ltd. All of their oil tankers were named after species of shells. They remained at sea until 2007. (HR12698.)

This view shows the prominent place of the shipyard in the harbour. In the foreground is the old poorhouse/Municipal Home. At the lower right are the terminal for the fertilizer plant and the storage tanks for Irving Oil. The Courtenay Bay breakwater reaches out toward Partridge Island with the still unfinished Negrotown Point breakwater at the right. At the centre right is a ship tied up to the Esso oil terminal at the Lower Cove. (HR1585.)

In 1983, the shipyard landed the contract to design and build 12 City-class Patrol Frigates for the navy. Construction began in 1985, and by 1996 HMCS *Ottawa* was the last to be completed. Three of the frigates were built in Quebec. The navy was provided with 12 operational ships backed by fully integrated logistics support throughout the life of the ships. (HR13110.)

The *Irving Ours Polaire* was one of several ships built for the Irving interests. Launched in 1964, the ship ended up with a few different owners before being scrapped in 2003. When the shipyard closed in 2003, the dry dock had built 126 vessels—from barges and scows, dredges, ferries, container and ore-oil carriers to fishing trawlers, an oil rig, and of course, several vessels for the Royal Canadian Navy. (Provincial Archives.)

Ten

THE FOLKS OUT EAST

Louis Eckebrecht is seen here with his cat in 1920. His mother was Margaret Foley, of the pottery family, and his father was Alfred Eckebrecht. He had two siblings—Joan and John. The Eckebrechts lived on Loch Lomond Road, and like many families with kids, family pets were the norm. The Eckebrechts also had a pet goat. Even during the early years of the 20th century, this area of the east side was still prone to see wild packs of dogs and herds of sheep and goats. (HR10835.)

In 1923, Samuel Arthurs and his father, Joe, of Hickey Road were participating in a public event at Fernhill Cemetery. At that time, they probably had no idea that a coffee and a donut would become such an important part of today's daily social intercourse. The number of vehicles in the background suggest that this was part of a Sunday event where families went to the cemetery to attend to their loved ones' graves and to have a picnic. (HR9820.)

During the winter of 1959–1960, these Grandview Avenue kids—(from left to right) Mike Dunn, John Bielli, Doreen Dunn, Ralph Mapplebeck and his sister Margo, and Pauline Dunn—slid down this hill many times. Within a few years, this became the site of the Saint John Institute of Technology, later the New Brunswick Community College. Paul (died 2005) and Marion Mapplebeck lived next door, moving to the area in 1951 and remaining until 2007. (Margo Mapplebeck.)

Tom Drummie and his friend Hatty Deshore may just be ready for a game of tennis at the community court at Drury Cove. Drummie married Winnifred Blair, the first Miss Canada in 1923. Tom was a well-known businessman, owner of the local newspapers in the 1940s and 1950s. The cove is named after the loyalist Drury family. The family home here was called Newlands, and in June 1880 it was the scene of one Drury killing his brother in a murder-suicide. (HR9801.)

In 1923, Marjorie Elizabeth Doig, the daughter of Fred Doig, a printer on Germain Street, went snowshoeing on Golden Grove Road. For some folks at this time, snowshoeing was probably the easiest form of winter travel on the east side. Today, almost 100 years later, there are still literally dozens of kilometres of wilderness trails in East Saint John, testament to the rural appreciation of longtime area residents. (HR4650.)

The Broderson family immigrated to New Brunswick from Denmark in 1928. In 1933, they moved to Saint John, where Terkild and Hertha rented the second floor of the house at 452 Rothesay Avenue, not far from the entrance to Fernhill Cemetery. The Brodersons lived in the house until the 1970s. Around the table in the mid-1950s are, from left to right, Edith with young Nora; her husband, Bob; Caroline; Kenneth; Hertha with Keith; Thorvald and his first wife, Marie; Jim; and Terkild. (Val Ward.)

Thelma Weir, daughter of Harold and Myrtle Weir, stands outside her home at 93–95 Thorne Avenue, just after World War II. Her costume certainly suggests that it was for a Valentine's Day party. The snow on the ground attests to a chilly February day. (HR 11816.)

The influence of Hollywood movies of the 1950s is evident in this early 1980s Halloween photograph of the Glen Falls Munn family. Mercer is an American Indian chief, and Terry is his wife. They were getting ready to go to the Saint John Racquetball Club on Chesley Drive for a party. Their son Andy stands behind his cousin Joey Geldart. (Terry Parlee Munn.)

These boys of the old Glen Falls School appear ready for a game of pickup basketball. Many of the schools in East Saint John were very much neighbourhood institutions. The students lived nearby, walked to school, and went home for lunch. After school hours, they played together and their parents socialized together. Only four boys are identified in this photograph—Mike Robichaud, Terry White, Bobby Storey, and Frank Leger. (Terry Parlee Munn.)

In 1947, Stu Trentkowsky and two friends climbed on the patio of the Jervis Bay Club on Bayside Drive, later home of the No. 53 Simonds Branch of the Royal Canadian Legion. The castle was originally the home of Allan McAvity, an engineer and businessman who operated the Canadian Independent Oil Company on Bayside Drive. He attended Harvard University, where he got his science degree, and he served as a Member of Parliament for Saint John from 1938 until 1940. (HR10852.)

In this 1930s image, Margaret Milne is doing something that no sane Saint Johner of today would do! She is skating on the Marsh Creek, in the area where the old CNR roundhouse was located. This was a relatively wide part of the creek. The neighbourhood kids also built rafts to sail up the creek toward Glen Falls. The really brave swam the one-handed Marsh Creek stroke, with the other hand pinching their nostrils. (Pam Milne-Vincent.)

Seen here is a 1942 Foley family concert at their home, Claymore Cottage, on Loch Lomond Road. Margaret (Foley) Eckebrecht is at piano; her son John is playing James Foley's violin; and his sister Joan is playing the recorder. Claymore Cottage still exists near the Jervis Bay Park on Loch Lomond Road. (HR10823.)

When Terry Parlee and her friend Elisabeth Feight were in the fifth grade, they turned into big-time business girls. They started babysitting for 50¢ an hour. Here Terry is holding someone whom she cannot remember, but next to her is her friend Kim Arsenault. They are standing behind Binghams store on the Glen Road. (Terry Parlee Munn.)

Arthur Pottle grew up in the Thorne Avenue neighbourhood and has fond memories of his youthful exploration of a rural East Saint John that, to a large degree, has disappeared. He has done his part to minimize the loss, as he loves to share stories of the delight of skating, swimming, skiing, and of wandering far and wide to the places that appear in this book. This image is of a 13-year-old Art, taken at Little Lepreau. His uncle was a forest ranger, and Art was able to travel around with him, no doubt learning a lot, especially the joys of storytelling. (Art Pottle.)